THE HISTORY OF THE
CROSSWORD

To Paul and Aram Paul

Published in 2016 by
André Deutsch
20 Mortimer Street
London W1T 3JW

ISBN 978-0-233-00491-4

10 9 8 7 6 5 4 3 2 1

Printed and bound by CPI Group (UK) Ltd, Croydon,
CR0 4YY

This book was previously published
as *The Centenary of the Crossword*

THE HISTORY OF THE
CROSSWORD
THE WORLD'S MOST FAMOUS WORD PUZZLE

Forewords by Richard Browne, *The Times Crossword Editor*
and the *New York Times'* Will Shortz

ANDRE
DEUTSCH

CONTENTS

Preface by Richard Browne
The Times Crossword Editor

So the crossword was only 50 years old when I got hooked on it in the 1950s! To my child's eye, there was something magic about the black and white squares, and I loved the way the words built up their interlocking pattern as I watched my grandfather fill in the answers. This started a lifelong interest and, when old enough, I started to enjoy the clues as well, as subtle little works of art on their own. It never occurred to me in those days that I might find myself earning a living from having such fun, even contributing to that icon of Britishness *The Times* Crossword.

Now that I am its editor, I first solve the puzzles as they arrive in my in-box, to put myself in the position of the reader. This way I can spot difficulties I might miss if I just checked clue against answer. I look out especially for possible alternative answers and spellings, and I identify and remove obscurities (basically anything I am not familiar with myself!). I also try gradually to update the ethos of the crossword while maintaining its traditions. We no longer assume readers' familiarity with Sophocles, Milton or remote corners of the Bible, but I do try to keep out too much popular ephemera, and to bear in mind that our crossword is now solved online all over the world.

At *The Times* we have a regular team of over a dozen contributors, and a small number of occasionals. As they all work independently, I often receive duplications of answers or clues and have to put puzzles on hold – I try to avoid repeating long phrases within a year or so. This can leave me at risk of running short; since no one is paid until well after publication day, there is not a universal enthusiasm for keeping me supplied well ahead, and I can find myself doing some awkward juggling.

I regularly receive unsolicited applications, often from established and excellent people, and it is unenviable to have to tell almost everyone that there is little prospect of being taken on, simply because of shortage of space. Many amateurs apply, but they rarely catch *The Times* style. The most common failing is poor surface sense (the clue not reading like a normal sentence or phrase). In my early cluing days this was a trap I fell into regularly, but I remember clearly when the penny dropped and I started making the surface reading the most important feature of my cluing. (For example, *Glance at the fixtures: not much on* – SCAN/TIES.) Occasionally a really brilliant crossword arrives out of the blue; though, alas, another pitfall is that a new compiler can produce one or two such good crosswords, but cannot step up to doing it regularly to a deadline. I do try to give everyone who writes to me at least a helpful and honest response.

The greatest delight of the job, apart from being able to do it from home at my desk overlooking the bird table in the garden, is the daily interaction with quirky and intelligent people, both those who supply and those who solve the puzzles. And it remains a thrill to be the first person to be solving all *The Times* crosswords, and trying to maximize the fun they will bring to our many thousands of solvers around the world.

Preface by Will Shortz
The *New York Times* Crossword Editor

It has been said that England and America are two countries separated by one language. We both speak English, nominally, but not quite alike. Sometimes, frankly, we don't even understand each other.

The same is true of our respective crosswords, only more so. While crosswords were alike on both sides of the Atlantic during the mid-1920s, when crosswords initially swept the world, very soon the British started adding twists to the clues — anagrams, homophones, puns, and assorted wordplay. Something about the British mindset won't leave anything 'obvious'. Soon a whole body of rules developed for cryptic crosswords (a term coined in America, by the way), which was adopted by all the leading crossword publishers in Britain.

Meanwhile, in America, the focus of crossword makers was increasingly to produce ever-more-sophisticated grids. Every letter in an American puzzle had to appear in two answers, across and down – a constraint not easy to do well. Our clues, though, stuck mostly to dictionary definitions, or at least straightforward hints to the answers.

Over time, Americans visiting Britain couldn't make heads or tails of their crosswords, and the British who saw our puzzles came to look down their noses at them.

Then maybe 25–30 years ago something interesting happened. Our respective crossword worlds started to merge again. The best American crosswords developed wordplay-related themes, sometimes as creative and maddening as anything in a British publication. Our clues became more creative, too. What the British call a "cryptic definition" became standard fare here.

And in Britain the so-called 'quick crossword' – a loose crossword lattice with synonyms and dictionary-type definitions of the answers – took hold, supplementing the regular cryptic puzzle in all the papers.

Since then crosswords haven't exactly come full circle, but the two worlds are now more alike than they're different. On each side of the Atlantic there's a large audience for puzzles with sophisticated wordplay, of one sort or another, and another audience for puzzles with straightforward clues. And with the help of this book, which explores the rich history of crosswords in Britain, America and beyond, maybe everyone can start to understand and appreciate the other side a little more.

Preface by John Halpern

"I hate you," he spat, hurriedly stuffing newspaper under his arm, and alighting from the train.

I guess I'd asked for it.

It turned out my fellow passenger had been familiar with the cryptic crossword puzzles I write for the UK's *Guardian* newspaper, under the pseudonym 'Paul'.

While his meticulously chosen words belied the slightly gauche nature of his departure, our brief encounter had been enough for me to ascertain that this was not an unscholarly man. I had it that he knew a thing or two about how to express himself, if not always verbally.

"Always good to see someone doing the crossword," I'd chirped. But this was not to be a chirpy exchange. I had interrupted him, pen poised, mid solve. Not the done thing. Not the done thing at all.

Though evidently not best pleased, being British the bespectacled gentleman simply furrowed his brow deep enough to plant tulips and sank deeper into his seat.

An introduction of this sort is all very well, but this was London; worse still the London Underground. In London we neither converse nor fraternize without the appropriately signed-off risk assessment forms and a solid exit strategy.

"You're doing well with Orlando," I observed, despite the absence of a prompt inviting me to continue. "He's a colleague of mine at the *Guardian*."

"Hmm," he muttered, and rose from his seat, possibly because his intended destination in London Bridge was approaching, but more likely because London Bridge provided his earliest opportunity for a swift getaway. With some purpose he jostled past me.

"I'm called Paul," I revealed.

Shamefully, I had been secretly hoping he would jolt to a halt, staggered simply to be in the presence of his favourite crossword setter, and that he would introduce me to the rest of the carriage as such.

But those were to be my last words to him. And "I hate you" his last to me.

But what was it that elicited such odium in a total stranger? Surely the passion of hatred comes only from having known someone intimately for many years. We had metaphorically been married far too long.

The occasion of marriage proper took place in the summer of 2011, and I inherited a lovely second family. Please refrain from hoots of derision, but my wife's family is neither into crosswords nor wordplay. Perhaps it's for this reason that I haven't yet informed her mum that MOTHER-IN-LAW is an anagram of 'Woman Hitler'. Perhaps.

Having said that, I suppose she has better things to do in her life than jumble the letters of 'mother-in-law' up and attempt to rearrange them. Thankfully the anagram is far from apposite.

However, what I fail to understand is how the first two children of my wife's twin brother have been named Levon and Sevan (Armenian names) without the realization by either parent that both names read backwards as English words. Furthermore, on informing the father of this quirk of verbal swivelling, I found myself feeling disappointed at his response of "Oh", rather than my hoped-for "Wow, that's amazing!".

Perhaps this says more about me, and the fact that sometimes I don't quite 'get' people who don't solve crosswords and those who don't enjoy word games. After all, there's so much fun to be had.

But when it comes to our little monochromatic pal, what exactly is it that we love so much about filling in our grid of squares?

Attending a recent football match in Brighton, my friend Claude and I discussed what it is that has us come back week after week. Why is it we are always primed with excitement and anticipation simply to sit outside, often in freezing weather, and watch 22 overpaid young men kick a lump of leather around a field?

"We need the escape from our daily lives," he suggested.

Football certainly gives us the opportunity every week to shout with joy, laugh or swear. We can grumble at the unfairness of the referee's judgment, delight in the silky skill of a deft pass or wince in horror at a crunching tackle.

Sometimes we win, sometimes we lose, but even if we are not kicking the ball ourselves, in a crowd of many thousands we are all together as one, part of something greater than ourselves.

"And it's about belonging," he added.

This observation in particular was ringing a bell, and my mind had drifted from the Amex Stadium towards another love of my life – another friend I could always turn to in fair weather and foul.

A crossword is a kindly uncle who would (almost) never let you down. And even if you did feel his words had been inappropriate, even if he had deceived or outwitted you, he'd still be there again the next morning, rejuvenated, washed and shaved – a fresh, clean and empty space of possibilities, inside which anything could happen.

So let's get to know that friend, that kindly uncle, a little better.

And let's go on a journey, a trip around the world, to meet the artists and scientists of our game. On our travels we will discover truly why we have our love/hate relationship with crosswords and their creators. Why is it we sometimes feel we would like to meet our torturer and buy him a drink, and on other occasions slap him across the face?

While this book gives a brief outline of crossword history, it's more about getting to know the people in the business; those who spend their time staring out of the window from converted home offices across the world, trying to think of an interesting way to clue POMEGRANATE, BUNG OR SUPERCILIOUS.

And it must be said, crossword people are passionate about their game.

In these pages we shall meet a man willing to murder over a crossword, crossword groupies and stalkers, and we shall experience love, veneration and spite among the online crossword community.

PREFACE

We'll talk to crossword editors across the world – what makes them tick, what makes them cross. And of course their teams of setters, those devious minds who've been delighting, exciting, informing and infuriating us all these years.

We shall discuss the fact that in 200 years of one national newspaper's existence, the issue sparking the largest number of complaints was the decision to demote the crossword from the back page to the inside back page, thus necessitating the kerfuffle of solvers having to wrestle with a large newspaper, folding and re-folding until comfortable across one's lap – not to mention the indignity of the crossword being considered less important than Sport or, perhaps worse still, Advertising (shudder).

This book is about our inherent nature to want to solve a problem; to be teased, to battle and lose many times in the hope that maybe next time we shall win.

Then, of course, there's the star of the show: the words.

As a creator of crosswords myself, it's my job to define the words. But surely it is the words we use – those we choose to write, those we choose to think and those we choose to speak, those we enjoy and those we don't – that ultimately defines us.

Oh, and the book has some crosswords in it. For consistency and ease of solving, I am reproducing them, where possible, in solver-friendly fonts and presentation, with clear lines and large friendly lettering, which wasn't always the case when they were first seen in print. Furthermore, in removing the visual imagery, I've left it to you to decide whether something feels dated or cutting edge. Generally, I've avoided weighing in too much with my unilateral opinion on the standard of each puzzle. As the solver, you are far better qualified to decide what you like and what you don't.

Many puzzles have been chosen for their historical significance, to illustrate a particular style, to introduce a particular crossword constructor, or a specific type of puzzle. Others have been chosen simply because they're fun.

And occasionally there are some (numbered) extra clues, often cited as favourites by various crosswording luminaries. The answers to these you can find at the back of this book.

So here we go. Let's get back to square one.

John Halpern, Brighton, 2013

SECTION 1:

THE HISTORY OF THE CROSSWORD

CHAPTER I
THE FIRST CROSSWORD:
How it happened and what happened next

It was on December 21, 1913 that the world was introduced to the crossword. Appearing in the *New York World*, it was compiled by a journalist from Liverpool called Arthur Wynne. Working in the wordsmith fantasist's 'Tricks and Jokes' department, Wynne was invited to come up with a new type of puzzle for Christmas. He dubbed it a 'Word-Cross', though by way of a typesetting error some weeks later it became a 'Cross-Word', and so the name stuck.

Opposite is a copy of that very first puzzle. The grid is more of the American style than British, with deeply interlocking words, rather than alternate black and white squares.

The diamond shape was borrowed from previously published word-based puzzles, but the drawing in of lines and boxes was Wynne's idea.

Clues are Horizontal and Vertical, rather than Across and Down. The word 'Dove' appears twice as a solution. There is some extraordinarily obscure stuff, and plenty of loose cluing.

But we can forgive him. Arthur Wynne gave birth to the world's most popular puzzle, which will be here long after people have tired of the 1–9 number filling that is Sudoku.

The journey of the crossword over the last 100 years is the journey of 100 years of fun with words, and we have a New York Liverpudlian by the name of Arthur Wynne to thank for it.

THE FATHER OF THE CROSSWORD?
Arthur Wynne was born on June 22, 1891, the son of George, editor of the *Liverpool Mercury*. Little is known of Arthur Wynne's early life, although the 1901 census shows him living (aged 9) at 100 Edge Lane, Liverpool, an address bulldozed in 2011 in order to make way for the Edge Lane widening project.

Definitely still standing to this day, not far away, is the Office and Printing Shed of the *Liverpool Mercury*. Dating from 1879, this would definitely have been the empire of George Wynne.

That building, in which the Father of the Father of the Crossword worked, has an arguably less than auspicious recent past. Currently the *Krazy House* nightclub, and advertised as 'Liverpool's biggest student night out', it is presumably an establishment with doors wide enough to welcome the city's most voluminous of scholars.

1. FUN'S Word-Cross Puzzle

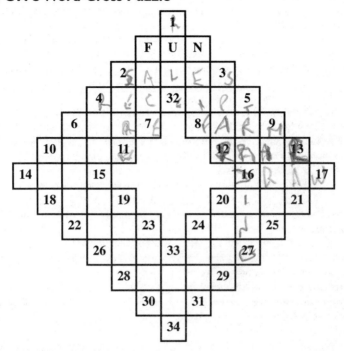

Fill in the small squares with words which agree with the following definitions:

2–3. What bargain hunters enjoy.	**6–22.** What we all should be.
4–5. A written acknowledgement.	**4–26.** A day dream.
6–7. Such and nothing more.	**2–11.** A talon.
10–11. A bird.	**19–28.** A pigeon.
14–15. Opposed to less.	**F–7.** Part of your head.
18–19. What this puzzle is.	**23–30.** A river in Russia.
22–23. An animal of prey.	**1–32.** To govern.
26–27. The close of a day.	**33–34.** An aromatic plant.
28–29. To elude.	**N–8.** A fist.
30–31. The plural of is.	**24–31.** To agree with.
8–9. To cultivate.	**3–12.** Part of a ship.
12–13. A bar of wood or iron.	**20–29.** One.
16–17. What artists learn to do.	**5–27.** Exchanging.
20–21. Fastened.	**9–25.** Sunk in mud.
24–25. Found on the seashore.	**13–21.** A boy.
10–18. The fibre of the gomuti palm.	

Given his dad's position, the newspaper industry had evidently been printed in indelible ink onto Arthur's mind, and he was to spend his entire working life in the world of publishing.

Forsaking home shores at the age of 19, Arthur settled in Pennsylvania with a job on the Pittsburgh Press. Incidentally, Wynne was also an accomplished violinist in the Pittsburgh Symphony Orchestra (which is perhaps unsurprising, for, as we'll see in our stroll through the world of crosswords, there seems to be a disproportionate number of musicians).

From Pittsburgh, Wynne soon progressed to the *New York World*, where he was asked to create his new puzzle, through which he was to make his name.

And while many of the elements that we consider part of a modern crossword had been around a long time before Wynne, the crossword in its present form has been attributed to Arthur himself. Although he never denied that his word-cross was anything other than similar puzzles he had seen in children's publications in England during his youth, he has been singled out as the puzzle's inventor. His crossword undoubtedly proved to be the spark for the crossword revolution that was to come.

Indeed, one could argue that the puzzle was far from original. I am indebted to translator Richard Fletcher for unearthing an Italian crossword-like puzzle from almost a quarter of a century earlier.

In 1890, Giuseppe Airoldi published his Milanese 'Parole Crociate' in *Il Secolo Illustrato della Domenica*. Really a word square, the puzzle had clearly defined Across and Down clues. However, it didn't catch on at the time.

AIROLDI'S PUZZLE OF 1890

Orizzontali: 1. Guai se l'onda mi varca o mi spezza 2. In Germania son acqua corrente 3. Ogni di quando il sole è morente 4. Cosi soglion le preci finir.

Verticali: 1. Sono un fiore di rara bellezza 2. Il medesimo in lingua latina 3. Quali frutti noi siamo, indovina! 4. Per la messe di là da venir.

In fact, much further back, the ancients had that innate need to create and solve puzzles. Magic squares and word squares with crossword-like elements have been found in the ruins of Pompeii, and 'cross-hieroglyphs' on ancient Egyptian monuments.

Furthermore, puzzles much like Airoldi's were being published in Britain and elsewhere during the nineteenth century. Roger Millington's marvellous book *The Strange World of the Crossword* describes a children's magazine called *St Nicholas*, running word squares with Across and Down clues as far back as 1880.

But whether his puzzle was 'original' or not, by the time of his death in Clearwater, Florida, in 1945 at the age of 73, Arthur Wynne would have been well aware of his crossword legacy, having been credited with instigating the phenomenal success story that is the (not so humble) crossword. So here's the history bit for the next handful of years after the first crossword: Nothing much happens.

In fact, it seems that for the next decade the *New York World* remained the only publication to run this new type of puzzle. Compositors hated the fiddly set-up of the squares on the page, and typesetting errors kept cropping up. When the *World* decided to drop the puzzle one week (for the crossword was published every Sunday, and was not to appear daily until 1924) staff were presumably quite surprised to be inundated with complaints. A following for the crossword had been accumulating rapidly.

And while, in England, it took until 1922 for the first crossword to appear (in *Pearson's Magazine*, where it was referred to as 'A new form of puzzle in the shape of a Word Square'), no one from either side of the Atlantic had yet fully capitalized on the latent possibilities of the crossword.

However, in 1924, two Americans by the names of Richard L. Simon and Max Schuster decided to launch a publishing business. 'Dick' Simon had been asked by his aunt for a little help with a crossword puzzle to which she had become addicted. She considered there should be a book of these published. And so the seed was planted, and Simon & Schuster was born.

A young Smith College graduate named Margaret Petherbridge and two of her co-editors at the *World* were asked by the publishers to write a book of puzzles. Then, seeking dealers to sell this compilation, Simon & Schuster received rejection after rejection, before eventually a buyer bought 25 copies out of friendship. That store alone was to end up selling many thousands.

The first book came with a pencil attached, and suggesting this was to become the latest fad, the Simon & Schuster advertising campaign read as follows:

1921 Coué
1922 Mah Jong
1923 Bananas
1924 The first crossword-puzzle book

In seeking outlets for their book, a few other stores had taken one copy each, just to see if it would be sold. But by the end of Day One of publication on April 10, 1924, and buoyed by some publicity from Franklin P. Adams, possibly the world's most famous columnist at the time, everyone had heard of this new puzzle and wanted a copy. Booksellers were madly ordering in bulk, and a year later Simon & Schuster had sold close to half a million copies.

Almost immediately there was a huge impact across America.

Doctors seemed anxious about solvers showing signs of 'neurotic traits', and were concerned about 'insomnia' and 'crossword patterns damaging the sight'. Authorities at the State Hospital for the Insane in Warren, Pennsylvania, found residents deeply engrossed in their new solving pastime. Further very welcome distraction was provided for those incumbent in one of the United States' most notorious correctional facilities, Sing Sing, NY, where prisoners awaiting execution were provided with puzzles and pencils to pass their final days.

By the close of 1924, scores of publications across America carried a puzzle. The nation was swept up in crossword fever.

And so, very quickly, was the world.

In **Italy**, although the 'parole crociate' of 1890 hadn't caught on previously, the first crossword proper appeared in 1925 in the *Domenica del Corriere*. The 'Indovinello' ('Riddle' or 'Enigma'), heralded the arrival of Italy's first 'cruciverba' (crossword), the word finding its way into Italian dictionaries by 1927.

In **Japan**, in keeping with the talent of the Japanese for taking and adapting ideas created in the West, the 'Ki Juji No Nazo', or 'crossword', was born, also in 1925. It is said that almost immediately the business communities in Tokyo and beyond sought to wrest solving tools from the fingers of their workers, many firms across the country banning crossword solving during working hours.

Arriving in 1925 in **Finland**, the crossword was first compiled under the pseudonym 'Suometar' or 'Finnish beauty', believed to have been the Finnish writer Seere Salminen, a woman reporting from London on the puzzle fever that had hit the city.

Ferdinand Lärns was the creator of the first puzzle in **Sweden**, with his 9×9 'Wordtwister' of 1924. Introducing the crossword to the Swedes, his preamble read:

"Here is a kind of brainteaser which is particularly popular in America ('the crossword puzzle'). Books of crosswords are published, people compete in the 'world crossword championship', and it is claimed that wealthy Americans forget their business deals when they get their hands on a crossword. They really are most fascinating. You don't really want to give up until you've got the solution sorted out."

And in **France**, the 'Mosaïque de Mystère' soon found its way onto the catwalks of Paris, stockings and dresses being patterned with black and white checks in honour of the in-vogue puzzle.

(continued on page 18)

2. Mosaïque de Mystère, 1925

1	2	3		4		5	6	7
8			■		■	9		
10		■	11			■	12	
	■	13	■		■	14	■	
15				■	16			
	■		■	17	■			
18	19	■	20			■	21	
22		23	■		■	24		
25								

HORIZONTALEMENT

1 Champêtre (9)
8 Favorable (3)
9 Chiffre (3)
10 Note (2)
11 Arme (3)
12 Préposition (2)
15 Fleur (4)
16 L'égal de quelqu'un (4)
18 Pronom (2)
20 Appel (3)
21 Note (2)
22 Arbre (3)
24 Particule d'atome (3)
25 Vive lueur (9)

VERTICALEMENT

1 Temps de verbe (9)
2 Conscience intime (3)
3 Note (2)
4 Personnage légendaire (4)
5 Terme de jeu (2)
6 Dépôt de liquide (3)
7 Détruit (9)
13 Fleuve (3)
14 Petit animal (3)
17 Vêtement (4)
19 Meuble (3)
21 La terre (3)
23 Négation (2)
24 Pronom (2)

(continued from page 16)

A student of Russian literature, *Guardian* crossword setter Sarah Hayes aka Arachne (see page 98) describes wordsmith Vladimir Nabokov's love of the puzzle, he being the man credited with introducing crosswords to **Russia**.

"Trying to scratch a living as an exile in Berlin in the early 1920s, Nabokov compiled 'a puzzle of crossed words' in Russian for the émigré newspaper *Rul'*. The Russian for 'cross' is 'krest', whilst 'word' is 'slovo', so – with an uncharacteristic lack of originality – he minted the neologism 'krestoslovitsa' for 'crossword', his politics plain to see in such clues as: 'A certain institution' (answer: GPU) [the GPU was a predecessor of the KGB], and 'What the Bolsheviks will do' (answer: DISAPPEAR).

"For Russians, the word 'cross' has heavily religious connotations, so whilst 'krestoslovitsa' was the name of choice for a crossword amongst émigrés, the now generally accepted Russian term 'krossvord' was introduced back in the USSR.

"Incidentally, Nabokov devotes Chapter 36 of *Ada or Ardor* to another word game played with a 15×15 grid. 'Flavita' (an anagram of the Russian word 'alfavit,' or 'alphabet') is 'an old Russian game of chance and skill based on the scrambling and unscrambling of alphabetic letters' which later, the narrator says, became popular again – under the name of 'Scrabble'. (Ada's set was given to her by a certain Baron Klim Avidov, an anagram of Vladimir Nabokov.) Similarly, another of the characters in the book, also making an appearance in *Lolita*, is Vivian Darkbloom."

Australia was to rely heavily on US and UK imports in the mid-1920s, evidenced by the lack of Australian terms appearing in early crosswords. Local commentators were unsure when the 'fad' would pass. Australian setters were rare, so newspapers sought to buy crosswords from readers, and puzzles began to have more of an Australian 'feel'.

And, with the crossword touring the world and the phenomenal success of Simon & Schuster, the work of Arthur Wynne was soon to arrive in **Britain**.

An American student touring Europe showed some puzzles by Wynne to C.W. Shepherd, manager of a British syndicating agency. Shepherd took them to the managing editor of the *Sunday Express*, Guy Pollock, who apparently received them with no great enthusiasm. However, Pollock took them home, and became converted. The first crossword in a British newspaper was published the following Sunday, in November 1924. The *Sunday Times* soon followed suit, but it was not until the *Daily Telegraph* got puzzling in 1925 that crosswords really began to take off on the eastern side of the Atlantic.

In 1925 Stanley Baldwin, crossword fan and prime minister, explained in a speech to the London Press Club the fact that "the newspaperman was helping me uplift Great Britain through the marvellous medium of the puzzle".

(continued on page 20)

3. Arthur Wynne's first 'British' puzzle
Sunday Express, UK, November 1924

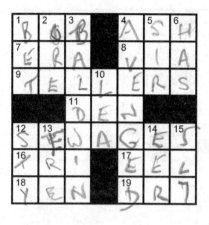

ACROSS

1 A coin (slang) (3)
4 A tree (3)
7 Period (3)
8 Through (3)
9 Counters of votes (7)
11 Cosy little room (3)
12 Drainages (7)
16 Meaning three (prefix) (3)
17 Snake-like fish (3) –
18 An oriental coin (3)
19 Parched (3)

DOWN

1 Wager (3)
2 Mineral substance (3)
3 Eminent political figure (7)
4 Inflected retribution (7)
5 A title (3)
6 Possesses (3)
10 Grassland (3)
12 Home of a certain animal (3)
13 Before (poetic form) (3)
14 Always (poetic form) (3)
15 Cunning (3)

Please note: in all puzzles reproduced in this book, for ease of solving, I have endeavoured to be consistent in format. For example, here the length of each solution is published (e.g. (3)), but in the original, this element was absent.

4. Crossword Puzzle No. I
The *Guardian*, January 5, 1929
(Contains the names of several well-known politicians).

(continued from page 18)

On July 30, 1925 the *Daily Telegraph* ran its first crossword, but those at the paper expected the craze to pass by very soon. To say the least, it didn't.

Offering two prizes of one guinea each, the *Guardian* first published a crossword in 1929, but it was only in 1930 that *The Times* of London finally succumbed to the 'American' craze and published its first puzzle in reaction to losing sales to their rivals at the *Telegraph*.

ACROSS

1 One of our Elder Statesmen (7)

6 Investigation (6)

10 A highly taxed commodity (3)

11 Whatever is fast is this (5)

12 Glaring, but, says the dictionary, also scandalous (8)

15 Those who remember the Boer War will remember this statesman (6)

17 Wet clothes are no use until they are this (5)

18 Describes poetry concerned with love (6)

20 Some fellows call themselves this (3)

21 A river in Russia and a gentleman in Spain (3)

22 When staff is added this fish is very plain (4)

24 Well known in the cotton mill (4)

26 An important pronoun (2)

27 A fairly common prefix and suffix (2)

28 A Locarno statesman (10)

32 An American author (3)

33 Where Cain went to (3)

34 The Tiger (10)

38 A bill sometimes becomes this (3)

39 Instrument favoured by Orpheus (4)

41 Men have sought its relics in Armenia (3)

43 To uplift (5)

45 Means the same (2)

47 Gets tidings of (6)

49 Insurrection (6)

50 Begins a famous Miltonic sonnet (6)

51 A 't'-less blow (2)

53 Abbreviation for Canadian province (2)

54 Compass point (2)

55 An orthodox Chancellor of the Exchequer (7)

56 A negative in more than one Latin language (2)

57 A French novelist or a London editor (6)

58 A Labour MP who became a Minister and left his party (7)

DOWN

1 The head of the Government (7)

2 Wing-shaped (4)

3 Military formations of the past revived in the Great War (7)

4 The vessel which the poet Gray called 'storied' (3)

5 Assigned fixed value to (5)

6 A politician as prominent in India as here (5)

7 Prepare a book for the press (4)

8 A Liberal leader (8)

9 A Tory ex-Chancellor (5)

13 Labour dislikes being called this (3)

14 Christopher not Joseph (7)

16 Part of the face (3)

19 One of Scott's heroines (6)

23 What new planets swim into (3)

24 Minister with historical feudal name (5)

25 To make one (3)

29 A once-familiar royal name (4)

30 A popular novelist (6)

31 The reverse of timid (8)

32 Less than anger (3)

35 A politician now in the City (7)

36 A member of the Labour Government (7)

37 A financier whose name has become proverbial in the Continent (7)

40 Won a notable by-election for Liberalism (4)

42 A Liberal politician prominent before and during the war who became an ambassador (5)

43 Peer who gave his name to a famous committee and edited a queen's letters (5)

44 One of Liverpool's MPs (5)

46 One of Manchester's MPs (4)

48 Very eager (4)

52 Heroine of a Greek legend (3)

THE MOTHER OF THE CROSSWORD

From 1914, in the *New York World*, Arthur Wynne had assumed position of editor, taking on new submissions and altering them as he saw fit. The crossword had appeared sporadically during the First World War, in a publication dominated by maps and talk of advances and retreats.

But returning to peacetime, there was little peace among typesetters at the *NYW*, still struggling with typesetting, and hating it. Error after error appeared, and the paper was deluged with complaints.

In 1921, when Wynne had had enough of all the errors at the *NYW*, he hired a young Smith College graduate, Margaret Petherbridge. Described by US crossword king Stan Newman as a 'crossword genius', Margaret is credited with instigating most of the features that remain a staple of American crosswords today.

Her puzzles soon became far more popular than those of Arthur Wynne.

At first Margaret was no crossword fan, simply seeking to further her career in publishing. Reportedly she would hardly glance at a crossword before selecting it for the newspaper. Complaints continued unabated, with Margaret dismissing those who took the time to write in as kooks.

But then, in 1922, columnist Franklin P. Adams (FPA) joined the staff, and his sarcastic remarks on the standard of the *NYW* puzzle, which he would deliver to her every morning without fail, started hitting home. Margaret had had enough. She started solving the puzzles.

It was then that the complaints seemed to make sense; instantly getting as frustrated and upset as her readers, she resolved to put it all right.

Things changed dramatically almost overnight. She began to standardize crossword formats, introducing a number after each clue to indicate how many letters the solution was to be. She began to discourage unwieldy crossword patterns, with symmetry of grids. The number of errors fell sharply.

It wasn't long before she was being approached by Simon & Schuster, and the first books of crosswords were born.

Margaret (now with the married name Farrar) remained at the centre of the puzzle world for many years, driving book sales and producing spin-offs, including puzzle books compiled from ideas by celebrities such as Irving Berlin and Harry Houdini.

CHAPTER 2
THE THIRTIES AND BEYOND

Through the post-Wall Street Crash, 1930s and the Depression, cash prizes in publications all over the world further increased the popularity of the puzzle.

According to Michelle Arnot in her entertaining *A History of the Crossword Puzzle*, "on January 29 1941 the *Chicago Daily News* reported that 15,000 people had descended upon the Chicago Public Library in a single day – all seeking answers to the same question."

Vandalism became prevalent among libraries across America. Pages were being torn out of relevant references, thus scuppering the chances of others to complete prize puzzles. There were long queues for the dictionary, and the telephones never stopped ringing. Pertinent reference books were kept by the library phone.

Something had to be done to stop this madness, and so policy at newspapers began to change to ensure there weren't any over-clever definitions, that solvers would remain in their homes, finish their puzzles easily, and not resort to the tearing out of pages – or of hair.

And so, as the 1930s progressed, puzzles became duller and the crossword's popularity waned.

But then World War II arrived – and people needed their crossword escape from the tragedies that confronted the world.

Right through the crossword boom of the 1920s, the decline of the 1930s and the upward trend of the early war years, the *New York Times* had remained one of the few top newspapers steadfastly refusing to publish a crossword.

However, during the war, the newspaper's publisher Hays Sulzberger had slowly fallen for the puzzle, and in 1941 a certain Margaret Farrar was hired. Under her experienced and committed editorship, the *New York Times* crossword would almost immediately become *the* quality crossword across the United States.

Back in Britain, crossword pioneers were being kept in the family – as with George and Arthur Wynne decades earlier, . That's the way things were done back then, evidently.

Adrian Bell, son of Robert, the editor of the *Observer*, had received no further education beyond school, but was to become the man responsible for launching the puzzle institution that is *The Times* Crossword.

His father had been asked by Robert Barrington-Ward, chief leader writer at *The Times*, if he knew anyone who could write crosswords. He didn't. But young Adrian, who protested that he knew nothing about crosswords, was famously given ten days to learn. Bell's first *The Times* crossword was published on February 1, 1930.

(continued on page 24)

5. First Crossword
The Times, February 1, 1930

Early setters of a new puzzle in a British magazine called the *Listener* included a gentleman by the improbable name of Derrick Somerset Macnutt and the Anglican clergyman A.F. Ritchie, the former writing under a reversal of his middle name 'Tesremos', the latter under 'Afrit'.

The puzzle, which runs to this day in *The Times* every Saturday, was to develop into arguably the toughest crossword of them all.

THE FIRST TIMES CROSSWORD

ACROSS

1 Spread unevenly (5)
4 Part of a Milton title (9)
10 A month, nothing more, in Ireland (4)
11 He won't settle down (5)
13 22 down should be this (9)
15 Cotton onto, so to speak (3)
17 Head of a chapter (4)
18 Denizen of the ultimate ditch (7)
21 Frequently under observation (7)
23 What's in this stands out (6)
25 Flighty word (4)
26 If the end of this gets in the way the whole may result (4)
27 Retunes (anag.) (7)
30 This means study (3)
33 Simply enormous (7)
36 There's a lot in this voice (4)
38 This elephant has lost his head (4)
39 A turn for the worse (6)
41 Done with a coarse file (7)
43 Red loam (anag.) (7)
45 This rodent's going back (4)
47 Makes a plaything with its past (3)
48 Wants confidence (9)
50 A mixed welcome means getting the bird (5)
51 This girl seems to be eating backwards (4)
52 The men in the moon (9)
53 A pinch of sand will make it dry (5)

DOWN

2 Heraldic gold between mother and me (5)
3 Out of countenance (7)
4 Upset this value and get a sharp reproof (3)
5 Intently watched (4)
6 In some hands the things become trumpets (5)
7 A religious service (8)
8 This horseman has dropped an h (6)
9 Sounds like a curious song (6)
12 This ought to be square (4)
14 Momentary stoppage (5)
16 Written badly (4)
18 Calverley's picturesque scholars carved their names on every one (4)
19 Site of 45 across (4)
20 Precedes advantage (5)
22 Parents in a negative way (3)
24 Used to be somewhere in France (5)
28 Happen afterwards (5)
29 Climbing instinct in man (8)
31 A terrestrial glider (4)
32 The final crack (4)
33 The little devil's on our money (3)
34 Simplest creature (5)
35 Time measurements (4)
36 Jollier than 4 across (7)
37 Ladies in promising mood (6)
38 Presents are commonly this (6)
40 Gets the boot (4)
42 Hail in Scotland may mean tears (5)
44 Works, but usually plays (5)
46 She's dead (4)
49 Only a contortionist could do this on a chair (3)

6. Crossword No. I
The *Listener*, February 26, 1930

This is the first *Listener* puzzle. In those days books were given as prizes to those who submitted a correctly filled grid to the newspaper. Setting the tone for years of mind-bending puzzles to come, there was only one correct entry on this occasion, from a Mr. I. Cresswell.

The blocked grid made an occasional appearance thereafter, but the barred grid (opposite) soon became the standard.

ACROSS

1 Spanish for *aubade* (8)

9 Musicians who possess this will draw the crowds (2)

11 The parent of the Sonata (5)

12 This music often figures in the broadcast programmes (5)

14 An opera by a Russian composer (10)

15 An English composer of anthems (4)

16 Quickly (6)

17 A semibreve in Common Time (10)

22 Singers sometimes have to do this (6)

23 The initials of a well-known English Musical Society (3)

24 Often with variations (3)

27 An opera by Sir Frederic Cowan (6)

29 Agitatedly (8)

30 Half of a famous opera (2)

31 Two parts on one stave (4)

32 An orchestra would be at sea without these (5)

34 For nine voices or instruments (7)

35 Initials of a musical society (3)

DOWN

1 The title of a ballad published before the war (7)

2 Caressingly (10)

3 An opera by Balfe (6)

4 Anagram of Old English word for a barrel organ (4)

5 A living composer (8)

6 A major (4)

7 An English composer (4)

8 Add three letters and this becomes a famous example of 12 across (4)

10 Popular at Covent Garden (6)

13 A non-musical term that might well sum up much of modern music (9)

18 The hero of one of Plato's myths (2)

19 Anagram of name of well-known promoter of concerts (4)

20 A flute player who taught at Brussels (5)

21 Conductor of a London choir (6)

25 Anagram of name of a baritone who first broadcast from Manchester (4)

26 The Paris Conservatoire stands in this (3)

28 First word of a famous Lenten hymn (4)

29 Last three letters of Christian name of a great composer (3)

32 Initials of a paper famous for its musical criticism (2)

33 A French word that is hardly ever stressed in a song (2)

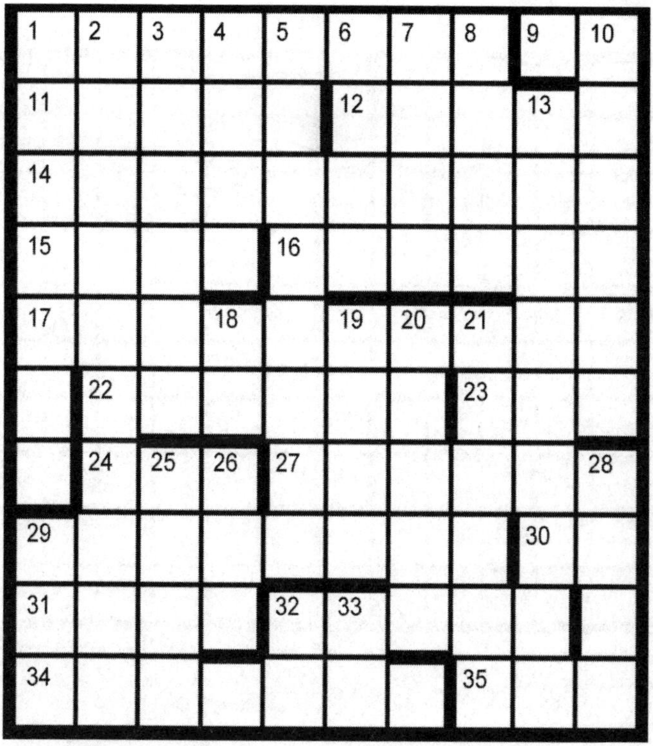

7. Knock Knock
The *Observer*, 1937

1	2	3	4	5	6	7	8	9	10	11	12	13
14						15			16			
17			18	19	20		21	22				
23		24		25					26	27		
	28			29		30				31		
32	33		34				35			36		
37				38	39		40					41
42		43	44	45		46				47	48	
49	50				51	52	53			54		
55								56				

So, in the 1920s and early '30s the crossword was firmly establishing itself in Britain, but where was the critical point at which the British style of crossword branched off from what we might term 'American-style' crosswords?

While cryptic 'rules' as such were not to be laid down until the 1960s, as early as 1926, strange goings-on were going on in South London.

Like Arthur Wynne and Adrian Bell, Edward (Bill) Powys Mathers was the son of a newspaper proprietor. Born in Forest Hill, South London, in 1892, educated at Loretto School in Scotland and then Trinity College, Oxford, he became a poet and translator of poetry. Some of his translations, like the crossword before him, found their way across the Atlantic and were set to music by the great American composer Aaron Copland.

(continued on page 30)

ACROSS

1 'Blank who?' 'Blank sitting down a minute?' (6)

7 'Blank who?' 'Blank 'd love to' (7)

14 'Blank who?' 'Blank no-how' (6)

15 rev. Lear had a runcible one (3)

16 Mulde contributes to me (4)

17 It's awkward to find the Lord Chancellor upside down in the street on a rainy day (5)

19 Plant obtainable from high ground overlooking a river valley (4)

22 rev. A theocracy (4)

23 Wore a russet mantle in Shakespeare (4)

25 Out of the eater came forth meat (4)

26 'Food for his ..., repasture for his den' (4)

28 A peep into taste (4)

29 See 33 (2)

30 'Blank who?' 'Blank terrible state of affairs' (4)

31 rev. 54 (2)

32 'Blank who?' 'Blank fool and caught a cold' (8)

35 (with 42) 'Blank who?' 'Blank the bounds of possibility' (4,3)

37 'Blank who?' 'Blank out and do it again' (6)

39 Vowels of 53 (2)

40 'Blank who?' 'Blank by a tiger' (5)

42 See 35 (3)

44 (with 48) Make a song about it (5)

46 'Blank who?' 'Blank ute tickle sing' (5)

48 See 44 (2)

49 'Blank who?' 'Blank, where is fancy bred?' (7)

53 Creeper formed of Edward and his son Charles (5)

55 'Blank who?' 'Blank pants, I make-a you another pair' (9)

56 rev. Better in character than in sugar (4)

DOWN

1 (with 9) 'Blank who?' 'Blank a wireless?' (3,2)

2 rev. Brownsea Island is in this harbour (5)

3 (with 9) 'Blank who?' 'Blank note of it' (3)

4 'Blank who?' 'Blank attack of itch' (4)

5 See 7 (2)

6 'Blank you?' 'Blank fool, aren't you?' (6)

7 rev. (with 5) Volume of a particle of dust (2)

8 'Blank who?' 'Blank I haven't had a drink all day' (8)

9 See 3 (2)

10 Room for a dislocated 25 (3)

11 See 12 (2)

12 (with 11) 'Blank who?' 'Blank and a small stout' (5,2)

13 (with 9) 'Blank who?' 'Blank ropodist called about my corns?' (6)

18 My small brother goes round the meadow (5)

20 rev. 27 (4)

21 I'm in from the sign (4)

23 rev. 'Blank who?' 'Blank pictures' (7)

24 rev. Impetus (4)

26 'Blank who?' 'Blank mow the lawn' (7)

27 'O Ararat there grows a vine; When ... from her bathing rose' (4)

33 Gets into a 26 ac. with 29 (3,2)

34 'Blank who?' 'Blank ephant never forgets' (4)

36 With or may say without if you are slow to learn (3)

38 'Blank who?' 'Blank who waits' (3)

39 My first is unchecked in 28, and my second in 13, 21, 23 dn., 52 and 55 (2)

40 (with 52) 'Blank who?' 'Blank did me wrong' (4)

41 More than the reverse of negative colours (4)

43 '... dim ... red, like God's own head' (3)

45 rev. There can be a chick before and a hen behind (3)

47 See 50 (3)

50 (with 47) Almost poached rat (5)

51 rev. First half of 41 (2)

52 rev. 39 dn. (2)

54 rev. 31 (2)

(continued from page 28)

Mathers, perhaps due to the ill health he suffered all his life, was a retiring type, and devoted to his love of words. According to his friends, Mathers disliked the American import of crosswords, and their 'inaccurate definitions', and so tried his hand at some more 'cryptic' clues. The Saturday *Westminster Gazette*, a literary magazine, ran these briefly, before the puzzles were taken up by the *Observer*. Mathers gave himself the name 'Torquemada' after the first Spanish Inquisitor-General, burner of thousands of fifteenth-century heretics. Thus Mathers himself become a pioneer in the art of torture.

Many of his puzzles were created in constructed verse, and others were written as a sort of narrative.

There's one from Torquemada on the previous page.

Imagine, for the 'Blank who?' clues, someone saying "Knock knock", someone else responding with "Who's there?" and the first person replying with a name – it's punning of which the great US puzzle constructor Merl Reagle, who we shall meet later, would be proud (I think!).

Torquemada crosswords became extraordinarily popular, up to 7,000 correct entries being received by the *Observer* every week, a mind-boggling number considering the level of difficulty of each crossword.

Early correspondence to Mathers from his masochistic followers suggested they were in raptures over his cluemanship, and often asked if he could make them even harder.

In fact it had been in response to this that the inquisitor had decided to erase all the black squares altogether, switching to the 'barred' puzzles on the previous page.

But in 1939 Mathers died, and D.S. Macnutt took over, taking the name Ximenes, one of Torquemada's successors as Grand Inquisitor of the Spanish Inquisition.

With his inventive writing style being greatly influenced by A.F. Ritchie (Afrit in the *Listener*), Macnutt published *Ximenes on the Art of the Crossword* in 1966. In it he laid down a set of principles he considered should be followed by all crossword setters, and this has influenced cryptic crossword setting to this day.

These rules included the use of a symmetrical grid, and a maximum and minimum number of 'unches' (unchecked letters), i.e. those letters appearing only in one word in the grid.

An attitude in response to loose cluing had been gathering pace during the 1950s, when a book of puzzles by Afrit included a statement now known as 'Afrit's Injunction'. It read: "You need not mean what you say, but you must say what you mean."

In his *Art of the Crossword*, Macnutt was to adhere to this idea, as he laid down his rules on producing quality clues.

Jonathan Crowther, Ximenes' successor from 1972 under the name Azed, sums up Ximenean principles on fair cryptic cluemanship as follows:

A good cryptic clue should contain:

1 A precise definition
2 A fair subsidiary indication
3 Nothing else

In the UK, the first *Financial Times* (*FT*) crossword appeared on March 21, 1966 during a period of great expansion of the newspaper under Sir Gordon Newton, editor at the time. Who set it? No records remain to tell us, though it may have been Irishman Patrick Cotter, the *FT*'s long-serving bridge correspondent (and renowned croquet player), one of just three compilers who set the puzzles for the next 13 years and more.

FT crossword editor Colin Inman, from whom we shall hear more later, describes the puzzle:

"A look at the first *FT* crossword from 1966 shows how clue writing has evolved over 40+ more years. No more than half the clues would be acceptable today; many lacked an adequate definition of the answer, while proper anagram indicators were mostly absent.

"Nowadays all cryptic clues contain a definition of the answer, either at the start or end of the clue; and this may be the easiest way in to a difficult clue: imagine that you are solving a synonym-only crossword with no cryptic content; this often works."

THE FIRST INDIAN CRYPTIC CROSSWORD
Commonwealth countries throughout the twentieth century would often use syndicated puzzles from *The Times* and the *Daily Telegraph*, amongst others, and also use a British-style grid. This practice has been the norm for decades in South Africa, Kenya and Australia especially, but there are always examples of good local setters who have established a following.

Admiral Katari was the setter of the first ever cryptic crossword in the *Hindu*, February 15, 1971.

He was one of the best Scrabble players in India, and when playing the game with his children, would be disappointed with a score below 700. He also would get angry if he saw anyone solving using anything but a pencil.

There's another of his on pages 34–35. It's a crossword with a very British feel. Solvers will find a misspelt solution at 17 down, but the puzzle is still solvable.

8. The First FT Crossword
The Financial Times, **1966**

ACROSS

1 The best brains are nearly all under canvas (6)

4 One means to get flowers (8)

10 Amusing or a dunce (9)

11 Acid answer (5)

12 Debatable (4)

13 Number prepared for transport (4-2-4)

15 "When he had __ wine to drink" (Gilbert) (7)

16 Arnold's was forsaken (6)

19 Specify in those who display crass ignorance (6)

21 Stop trembling (7)

23 Exaggerated performance (10)

25 Rest in post-operative period (4)

27 Correct girth (5)

28 Coloured fisher shows sign of departure (4,5)

29 A fool in the game is annoying (8)

30 Dodgy vessels (6)

DOWN

1 Time-serving barbers (8)

2 Capitalists? (9)

3 Standard catechistic reply to nominal enquiry (4)

5 Remedy with alcoholic base (7)

6 But not in *Ward 10* (4,6)

7 Home of Heracles' lion (5)

8 Meetings that end in agreements (6)

9 "He did his very best to make the billows __ and bright" (Carroll) (6)

14 Watch the stakes for committee members (10)

17 Stop at sea renegades (9)

18 Army and Westminster types dry up as show directors (8)

20 Remarkable without entertainment (7)

21 If you hold it you can't give it (6)

22 Welcomed to bridge by trio (6)

24 Agree to be a bore (5)

26 Knocks up a yard (4)

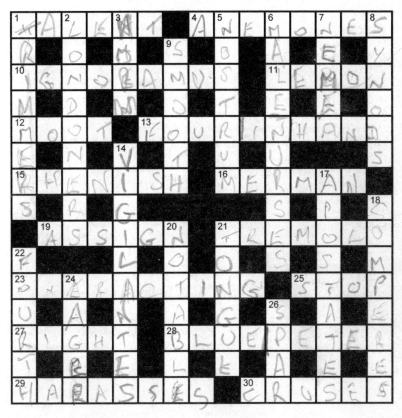

Reprinted with the kind permission of the *Financial Times*.

9. Crossword No. 1000
The *Hindu*, October 17, 1974

ACROSS

1 Quite knowing about the song (6)

4 Gathering of legislators (8)

10 Fold back material insurance body claimed (9)

11 His hoard gives him utmost pleasure (5)

12 Lured 8 in the final phase (7)

13 Result of the debutante's first party? (7)

14 Left the donkey nothing but the rope (5)

15 It is upsetting when these are roused (8)

18 Swimmer's mate known for her loud mouth (8)

20 Miss Gardner has one pound that is of use (5)

23 The walk that's seen on a dance floor in London (7)

25 Eight in trouble in trade name that may take up the slack (7)

26 Headless peer that is weird (5)

27 Deviation that makes Lincoln wrongly carry about a name (9)

28 Such men are certainly not officers (8)

29 Satisfy that excuses are up to the point (6)

DOWN

1 Once in favour of myself on the railway (8)

2 I married favourite with America as the incentive (7)

3 It just about provides a bare covering (9)

5 Offend one with a measure in readiness (4,2,4,4)

6 Half of them came up with the insect (5)

7 Singing voice that has nothing on the instrument (7)

8 Tricky delivery from northern England (6)

9 Advantage accompanied by worry calls for caution on the crate (6,4,4)

16 Opening in short month on the range (9)

17 It is a game of patience to get the source of wealth (8)

19 I'm married before the examination. It's very sinful (7)

21 Aerial worker meets the girl coming back (7)

22 Claim support in drink (6)

24 The lady takes divergent points against the odds (5)

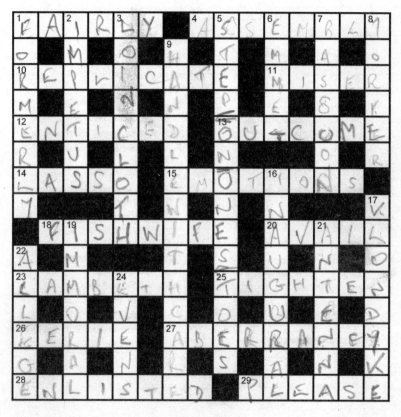

Reprinted with the kind permission of the *Hindu*.

10. Orlando crossword
The *Guardian*, 1978

And here's a *Guardian* cryptic from 1978, very accessible and solvable by today's standards.

ACROSS

1 Kinsman has article that's impure (7)
5 Mean girl in mature surroundings (7)
10 Food taken back in town (4)
11 No-one returns after tax is put on US city for renewal (10)
12 Amatory hero tickled some (6)
13 Sport for youth-leader playing around hilltop (8)
14 Does evident disagreement bring him to court? (9)
16 Group of soldiers or policemen surrounding king (5)
17 Out of a Scottish river (5)
19 Offers to support and love lass, perhaps (9)
23 Hawthorn's first in flower – the first in the field (8)
24 A small insect with eastern relative (6)
26 Actor embraces former railwayman (10)
27 Principal sea force (4)
28 Cultivating fruit on top of greenhouse (7)
29 Capital radio receiver for ruling clique? (4-3)

DOWN

2 Non-combatant in new Renault (7)
3 Settle for what Sunbeam provides (5)
4 Fruit causing Capri to break down (7)
6 It may follow Allegro or Vauxhall to church (6)
7 Lots come outside to reverse Rolls (9)
8 Minor? Certainly not! Is this how stock of Hillman is increased? (5-2)
9 Part-exchange for Avenger? (2,3,3,2,3)
15 Friends fix a Mini up with internal tin-opener (9)
18 Danish girl sticking her head in Opel and back of Lancia (7)
20 Rapier and E-type – terribly plain (7)
21 Reliant styled for convenience (7)
22 Instrument for Chrysler? So we hear (6)
25 How mother gets on, reversing the Land Rover? (5)

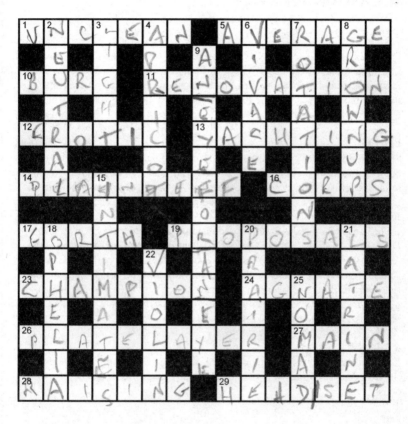

First published in the *Guardian* newspaper.

CHAPTER 3
CROSSWORDS IN RECENT YEARS, ALL AROUND THE WORLD

FRANCE
French crosswords are not always square and are smaller than those from the UK. In fact, they are sometimes not even symmetrical. And two-letter words in the grid would probably be frowned upon among British cruciverbalists in much the same way that the French would frown upon the discovery of Cheddar in their baguettes.

ITALY
I lived in Rome briefly during the 1990s; in fact my first *Guardian* puzzle was published while I was in the capital teaching English as a foreign language. Some of the first crosswords I wrote were written while seated under the colonnades of St Peter's Square, the joke in my head being that, given my pseudonym, I was John-Paul III.

The hunger for puzzles in Italy is fed mainly by *La Settimana Enigmistica*. Founded in 1932, the magazine, which contains number puzzles and riddles too, also runs variations on the standard crossword (whose grid is of the American style). There are also 'incroci obbligati', crosswords with clues given in random order, and no diagram, the solver being asked to construct the grid too. Italian puzzles are generally larger than in France, the usual dimensions being 13×21 squares, with two-letter words also allowed.

POLAND
Extraordinarily, nouns are the only words allowed in Polish puzzles, though the British style of grid with more black squares allows for easier puzzle construction.

JAPAN
Japan has three writing forms, hiragana, katakana and kanji, those three rarely mixing in any crossword puzzle. One syllable (katakana) is to be written into each white square, so grids tend to be smaller than in other languages.

ISRAEL
Modern Hebrew is normally written with only the consonants; vowels are either understood or appear as diacritical marks. This can lead to ambiguities in the entry of some words, and compilers generally specify that answers

are to be entered in either *ktiv male* (with some vowels) or *ktiv haser* (without vowels). Further, since Hebrew is written from right to left, but Roman numerals are used and written from left to right, there can be an ambiguity in the description of lengths of entries, particularly for multi-word phrases. Different compilers and publications use differing conventions for both of these issues.

UNITED STATES

The crossword continues to delight and perplex its fans, with its brilliant construction and marvellous themes – sometimes even topical. None more so than a crossword published on November 5, 1996. Written by Jeremiah Farrell, it is cited by *NYT* crossword editor Will Shortz as his "all-time favorite".

November 5, 1996, happened to be the day of the US presidential elections. A number of down clues, all of which which intersected with one particular 7-letter across entry, had alternative solutions. For example 'Black Halloween animal' could have been BAT or CAT.

This allowed for the solution to 39 across, the clue for which read 'Lead story in tomorrow's newspaper (!) with 43 Across' – the answer to 43 across being 'Elected' – to be either CLINTON or BOB DOLE.

On the morning of November 6, the *NYT* was inundated with bewildered and irate puzzle solvers, many asking: "How on earth did you know?" and many others complaining: "You got it terribly wrong!"

BRITAIN – AND A VERY BRITISH OBSESSION

And of course, deeply ingrained within the modern culture of Commonwealth countries is another, sometimes perplexing, pastime that's just as gentle and as bruising in equal measure.

Cricket is so deeply ingrained into British crosswords that it comes as a surprise when what appears to be a reference to cricket isn't about cricket at all.

A good example is this:
'Centuries for MCC, for example (8)'

This clue, by Brendan, appeared in the *Guardian* in May 2013 and, because MCC is the most famous cricket club in the world and is the owner of, no less, the laws of cricket, it must (surely?) have a solution that is about cricket.

Sadly not so. While the solver is busy trying to work out how you get 'hundreds' (for which 'centuries' would be a perfectly decent definition) out of a subsidiary indicator of 'for MCC, for example' or tries to think of a way in which the clue might be a fiendish example of the '& lit.' type (further explained later in this book), the clue in fact has nothing to do with cricket. It is about mathematics, and the solution is TWELFTHS, which centuries are to the twelve 100s indicated by the Roman numerals MCC.

11. The *Mint* of Delhi Crossword
By Tony Sebastian, April 1, 2011

"Since it's April Fool's Day, starred clues have vague definitions (but a common theme unites them). See you all at the Wankhede tomorrow."

[Author's note: for the uninitiated, the bamboozled and the uninterested, the Wankhede is the cricket stadium of Mumbai.]

ACROSS

1 *Supply six at first – this guy can do that (8)

7 Odes to great matches? (11)

8 South African player in England, perhaps – rag transformed in place making riches (7)

9 Relic for South African going back home (3)

10 Spoil everything without taking one single (3)

12 *Commotion surrounds crazy lash by this player (7)

15 Miscued shot giving a first innings advantage? (7,4)

17 *Bowler to plant ball and catch also (8)

DOWN

1 I've to struggle and compete (3)

2 Regretting decision to leave Lasith's first (5)

3 *He ran quite terribly because he's a fast bowler (5)

4 Applause for England's hundred – tardy, ends abruptly (5)

5 Perhaps Watson's girl? (4)

6 *Almost the perfect person, has a Church built in his name (6)

8 *He's slipped one past the wall (6)

11 Close to the left side (4)

12 Cricketing shot played off and on (5)

13 Indian cricket film losing academy's first – it's all at sea (5)

14 Cricketer Matthew is left without a name (5)

16 Self-importance caused England's exit (3)

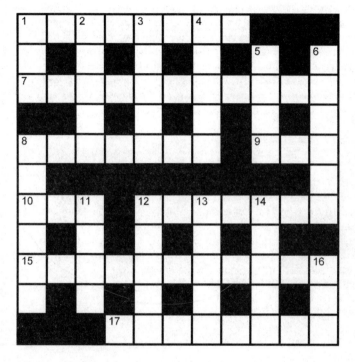

Reprinted with kind permission of the *Mint* newspaper.

But more often the clue will be about cricket, and the sport has such a rich and varied vocabulary that it must surely be impenetrable to those who have grown up without the game. In the mad world of cricket LEG is ON which is not OFF. SILLY means CLOSE or SHORT, and is the OPPOSITE of DEEP. COVER is a fielding position unless it means protection provided by a fielder who is in the DEEP and therefore not SILLY. And so on. Throw that into the anarchy that is, in any case, the English language and you have the recipe for hours of fun, or of torment, as you prefer.

From time to time there is debate about whether cryptic crosswords as we know them are quintessentially 'English' (or possibly 'British') and there is a case to be made that the defining English feature is the inclusion of cricket. Araucaria, the pre-eminent setter, called it 'The jumping game (7)' (CRICKET) in a *Guardian* puzzle some years ago and the game seems to appear in almost every puzzle set in the UK, if only by implication. Take this example from Rufus:

Length of time in the middle (10).

'In the middle' is a phrase that means something particular to cricketers – the time he or she spends batting – and they will read it that way, but in fact the clue, like TWELFTHS above, has nothing to do with the game. The solution is CENTIMETRE and the definition is 'length', which you get by putting TIME in CENTRE.

But so be it. Perhaps the rest of the world will have to accept, as Bunthorne once said, that "With which to admit in France that's just not cricket. (8)". PASSPORT, don't you see? Or "pas sport", as the French might say. But try getting a cricket fan to admit that.

SECTION 2:

TYPES OF CROSSWORDS,
THEIR RULES AND SOLVING TIPS

CHAPTER 4
THE QUICK

The 'Quick' crossword, sometimes called the 'Easy' crossword, the 'Concise' or perhaps the 'Straight' firstly makes the assumption that the solving will be Quick, Easy, Concise or Straight. It often is – but it is often not.

This depends, of course, on the writer of the puzzle, and from which side of the bed he has emerged on that particular day. Whether gruntled or disgruntled as he or she wakes, it is the job of the setter to provide definitions throughout that can lead to only one specific answer, and no other. A solver being left with _USTARD and the clue 'Hot yellow sauce (7)' just won't cut the custard. Publications and freelancers alike work from their dictionaries of choice – for example, *Merriam-Webster* in the USA, and *Chambers* in Britain.

For the last ten years or so, pretty much everyone around the world has used crossword setting software, which allows the setter to choose a grid, fill it at the press of a button, lock in words he likes from the computer's database, empty the rest of the grid and then autofill again and again until the grid is filled – after which the clues are written. My clues for the *Guardian* Quick Crossword are sometimes definitions I know off the top of my head, but they're usually double-checked via *Chambers*, *Collins* or the *New Oxford Dictionary*. Sometimes I also use a thesaurus for ideas, but these are often imprecise definitions, of course.

There are three 'Quick' setters for the *Guardian*, and we set them on a three-week-on, six-week-off basis, so 18 Quick Crosswords in a row will probably be by the same setter, the same grid patterns numbered 1–18 recurring tri-weekly. Currently those three are Michael Curl, John Dawson (aka Chifonie) and myself.

Before the turn of the new millennium, grids would be filled in by hand, the setter often aided by books listing words of every length, and with every combination of possible letters for remaining spaces.

For example, if left with A _E_T, various 'completer' books such as those produced by Longman and Chambers would offer the options ADEPT, AGENT, ALERT, ALEUT, AMENT, ANENT, AREN'T and AVERT, via flicking to the list of five-letter words beginning with 'A'.

With a 'Quick', much like any crossword, it's all about the words. Words elicit imagery in the mind, and I firmly believe that positive and vibrant words can set up the solver's day. Creating a crossword theme on, for example, diseases is, understandably, discouraged.

Furthermore, experience tells me that a puzzle relatively free of plurals, words ending 'ed', '-ing' words, and those with the suffix 'ness' create more energy in the solver.

QUICKS 1 AND 2

S		M		U		H			D		P		L
T	R	O	U	N	C	E			I	R	A	T	E
A		R		T		L			A		R		T
T	R	I	E	R		L	I	M	I	T	E	D	
E		B		U				E				O	
	O	U	T	S	E	T		T	H	R	O	W	
H		N		T		I		R		E		N	
E	N	D	O	W		C	R	I	S	P	S		
P			O			C		O			O		
T	H	E	O	R	E	M		A	C	R	I	D	
A		X		T		I		L		T		D	
D	E	A	T	H		R	E	L	I	E	V	E	
S		M		Y		E		Y		D		R	

A		U		E		S		D		E		S
C	O	M	E	D	I	C		R	U	R	A	L
I		B		G		A		A		O		E
D	E	R	B	Y		N	I	G	H	T	I	E
I		I			D		S		I			K
T	W	A	N	G		A	Z	T	E	C		
Y			A		L		E					B
	S	C	R	A	M		R	I	F	L	E	
G		N		L		O			A		Q	
I	T	A	L	I	A	N		B	I	J	O	U
M		Z		C		G		L		I		I
M	U	Z	A	K		E	P	I	S	T	L	E
E		Y		Y		R		P		A		T

Have a look at the two grid-fills on the previous page, and see how you 'feel' after tasting the words for Quick 1 compared with Quick 2. Roll the words around your tongue. Allow your mind to take you on a journey. Which do you prefer? There is no right answer to this.

American-style grids, given their close-knit words, more often than not end up with a number of non-dictionary words, with plenty of abbreviations and variant spellings. 'Abbr.' indicating the former, and 'Var.' the latter. Roman numerals also crop up as solutions, perhaps clued as, for example 'VI × II', answer 'xii'. Compass points are frequent too, being suggested by 'New York to Washington dir' for example, for 'ssw'. Non-dictionary solutions and 'Complete the phrase' answers are also allowed, such as 'GO TO SCHOOL' and 'I DON'T', clued as 'Attend classes' and '___ care'.

In Amy Reynaldo's excellent *How to Conquer the New York Times Crossword Puzzle,* the author takes us through the process of solving for Easy, Medium and Hard puzzles respectively:

"'Easy' refers to Monday and Tuesday puzzles. The difficulty level ratchets up a bit heading into Wednesday and Thursday, while you might find yourself at first stymied by the heightened challenge of a Friday or Saturday puzzle."

Reynaldo also describes how the puzzle constructor might trick you in his or her cluing. For example, the first word of a clue is always a capital, so this fact can deliberately be used to lead the solver up the garden path. The examples she gives you are 'Hamlet's cousin' as a clue for VILLAGE, 'People person' referring to an EDITOR and 'Frost lines' giving you VERSE, lines from poet Robert Frost.

Where the solver of the *NYT* puzzle might also get stuck is in what the author describes as 'Odd Letter Combinations'. Consecutive 'QTY' letters might suggest the solver has made a mistake. But the solution GQ TYPE, the sort of man who one might associate with *Gentlemen's Quarterly* magazine, is the kind of solution that may crop up in the *NYT*.

Another situation in which the solver has been known to slip up (and why a pencil may be recommended, rather than a pen!) is the 'Two-Good-Answers Trap'. Some constructors will deliberately set out to give you more than one possible entry – the example quoted in this book being 'Georgia neighbor' which could be ALABAMA or ARMENIA. The solver may have already entered an 'A' at the beginning and the end before confidently entering the wrong option.

In British-style grids, the setter must be extra wary of this happening, as there are far fewer letters 'checked' by other solutions.

And for Reynaldo, cheating – at least at first – is OK.

"Cheat, by looking up answers when you first start in order to familiarize yourself with crossword conventions in cluing and fill. As you become adept at solving without outside aids, you can wean yourself off them."

And to reiterate, do start by choosing Monday or Tuesday puzzles. To illustrate this, the author gives this example:

"One of the most common 4-letter answers is AREA.

"Monday or Tuesday clues for this might be: 'Region' or 'District'.

"On a Wednesday or Thursday, 'It may be grey' or 'Plane measure' might appear. By Friday and Saturday the more obscure synonyms are evident: 'Purlieu' or 'Vicinage'."

And then there are the Sunday puzzles. Reynaldo describes these as being of around Thursday difficulty, but they may take longer to solve, as they are larger grids. It is only on a Sunday that the puzzles have a title, which hints at a theme.

Here, I have just scraped the surface of the solving process, Reynaldo's book is very thorough, a step-by-step guide to the process, with many examples from the *New York Times*.

To illustrate, on the following pages are four puzzles from the American Crossword Puzzle Tournament, kindly supplied by *NYT* Crossword Editor Will Shortz.

12. Monday: Buzzwords
by Lynn Lempel

This challenge is surprisingly stiff.

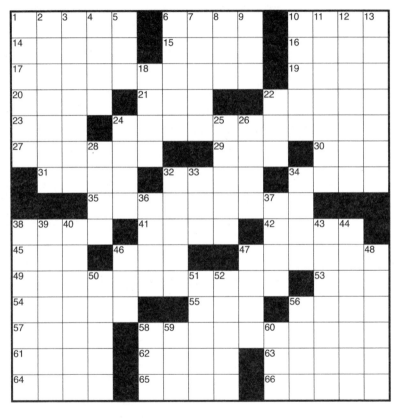

THE NEW YORK TIMES

ACROSS

1 Bumbling
6 Part of P.T.A.: Abbr.
10 Historian's purview
14 Film feature once Dorothy gets to Oz
15 Cook some cookies, say
16 '___ la Douce'
17 College course that covers the classics, colloquially
19 Cause to stumble
20 "Of course!"
21 Ballerina's support
22 Large amount
23 Hula accompaniment, for short
24 Subtropical weather system in the Atlantic
27 Eat like a bird
29 Harrison who played Professor Higgins
30 Earth-related prefix
31 Earth
32 Hourly pay
34 Prince Charles's sister
35 Some offensive linemen... or what 17-, 24-, 49- and 58-Across could be said to have?
38 'Ben-Hur' setting
41 Clumsy sorts
42 People who cry foul
45 Formula ___ (type of auto racing)
46 Retail tycoon Walton
47 Find out about
49 Situation that might lead to a grand slam
53 Suffix with magnet or quartz
54 Hawke of "Dead Poets Society"
55 PETA taboo
56 Tennis trailblazer on a 37¢ stamp
57 Trounce
58 Attacked with incendiary devices
61 'Julius Caesar' garment
62 Superstar, to fans
63 Tractor name
64 "Immediately!"
65 Head honcho
66 Twisted smile

DOWN

1 Freezes over
2 Chant outside a modern power plant, maybe
3 Spanish painter known for his elongated figures
4 Barber's striped attention-getter
5 Prefix with cycle
6 Detest
7 Massachusetts town with a witch museum
8 Compete in the giant slalom, e.g.
9 Earn as profit
10 Sales spiel
11 Summon to court to answer a charge
12 Teensy amount
13 One of a pair for Astaire
18 "Keep it," to a proofreader
22 Lisa Simpson's instrument, for short
24 Neighbor of Java
25 Impulses
26 Celebrity chef Paula
28 Toy on a string
32 Company that makes 43 Downs
33 Org. that hunts smugglers
34 On the briny
36 Soccer score
37 1857's ___ Scott decision
38 Key Supreme Court vote upholding the Affordable Care Act
39 Bingeing
40 Off one's rocker, to a yenta
43 Toy used in disc golf
44 "I showed you!"
46 Nine-digit ID
47 Parsley or basil
48 Backyard bird enticement
50 Trouble persistently
51 Bushy dos
52 Confrontations at 20 paces, say
56 Grace finale
58 "Oh, I loved your fruitcake," maybe
59 Wedding words
60 Takes too much, briefly

13. Wednesday: Short Breaks
by Mike Shenk

This one will take a little time.

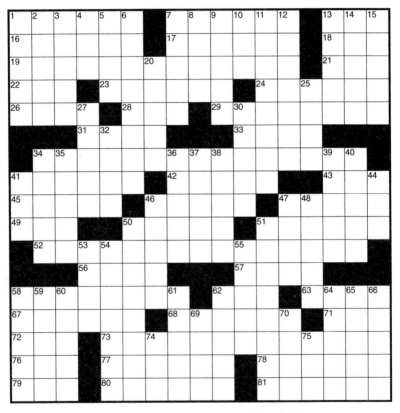

Reprinted with permission © 2013 American Crossword Puzzle Tournament.
(www.crosswordtournament.com)

ACROSS

1 Service man?
7 Marbles, so to speak
13 Prefix akin to equi-
16 'True Blood' waitress
17 Stable model
18 Short time added to two Across answers
19 Slightly better-than-average motorists?
21 Bringer of wisdom, some say
22 Cut (off)
23 Decisive step
24 Coy answer to "Will you?"
26 Words of approximation
28 Swindle, in slang
29 Empathize with
31 "Like that'll ever happen!"
33 Sighed word
34 Comment that's really cutting?
41 Passionate
42 More ticked off
43 Ending with depend or correspond
45 'Bullets Over Broadway' Oscar winner
46 Placed
47 He's won more acting Emmys than any other man
49 "As lightly her form bounded over the ___": Shelley
50 Frenetically busy
51 It turns litmus blue
52 Something passed that's too hot to handle?
56 Hypocritical talk
57 Pointer's word
58 Ready to be shot, perhaps
62 ___ jeans
63 Marco Polo's heading
67 Minimal
68 God of the underworld
71 Kitten coat
72 One of the Peróns
73 Advice for fearful rocket travelers?
76 Short time added to two Across answers
77 Provide with an improved view, perhaps
78 May Day baby, e.g.
79 Antlered animal
80 Catherine who owned a barn in Chicago
81 Is out

DOWN

1 Cellist Casals
2 Mail, for example
3 Minor mistakes
4 Top rating, at times
5 Encumbrance
6 Limit
7 Cash substitute
8 In need of irrigation
9 "When pigs fly!"
10 Ephemeral sculpting medium
11 Best-selling album of all time
12 Respectful reply
13 Pol's concern
14 Glimpse
15 ___ a customer
20 Go with the flow
25 Birth announcement beginning
27 Fertile spots
30 Like some 70-Downs
32 Dispatched
34 Short-lived
35 Shining example
36 Walt Whitman's '___ the Body Electric'
37 "___ I see you first!"
38 Singer/pianist Buddy
39 Kidney-based
40 Ring
41 Saddler's tool
44 Half of hex-
46 Health, to Henri
47 Jessica of 'Sin City'
48 Diamond-shaped fish
50 Medieval musician
51 They're beyond belief
53 Pine
54 Conductor
55 Alamogordo's county
58 Bigger than big
59 Place for a piercing, perhaps
60 Limited support?
61 Salt's heading
62 Like some pockets
64 Previously, poetically
65 Rooster's cue
66 Lock
69 Capital symbol
70 Creature that may be 30-Down
74 Purpose
75 Pool tool

14. Friday: Take Five
by Patrick Blindauer

But take each only once.

Reprinted with permission © 2013 American Crossword Puzzle Tournament.
(www.crosswordtournament.com)

ACROSS

1 One of about a billion believers
6 Drop down?
10 Ran into
16 Bagel choice
17 Word that may come before itself?
18 "Airplane!" heroine
19 "Macbeth" prop
21 Pet toy filling
22 Some buglers
23 Rossi of 'Sons of Anarchy'
24 'Rhythm ___ Dancer' (1992 Snap! song)
26 Cover
27 Common word that's sometimes contracted
28 Group with primates

31 Snap, maybe
34 Wanting for nothing
35 As easy as falling off___
36 A hose comes out of it
38 Poetic time of day
40 Triangular part of a house
44 Waggle dance waggler
45 Get absorbed
47 Postal label
48 First name in the Motorcycle Hall of Fame
50 Figure set by the Federal Reserve
52 'Forever, ___'(1996 humor book)
53 Suburb of Boston
55 Timorous
57 ___ the Clown
58 Neighborhood of New Orleans
59 Rock band?
60 Oscar-winning actress who is a practicing 1-Across
62 Stuff in a muffin, maybe
64 When repeated, a "Teletubbies" character
66 Wipe out
67 Lightheaded people?
71 Bump hard
72 Course for beginners?
73 Certain game win
74 "Just joshing"
76 Film fx
79 Rant about, slangily
81 Washington and others
84 Wait on
85 It's waved at the Olympics
86 Vehicle with a hyphen in its name
87 Passes, with "away"
88 Source of the word "brogue"
89 Didn't disturb

DOWN
1 She wrote the line "His truth is marching on"
2 Like some flights: Abbr.
3 Cause for a Band-Aid
4 Animated exclamation
5 Frees, in a way
6 Pack ___
7 High, in a way
8 Photocopier tray: Abbr.
9 Do, musically
10 Product displacement?
11 With 37-Down, menu phrase
12 What the Australian TV show "Blankety Blanks" was based on
13 Trivial
14 Tech debut of 1946
15 Asset for a team
20 'Voi ___ sapete' ('Le Nozze di Figaro' song)
25 Hour, day or week
27 Writer Rand
29 Hailee nominated for an Oscar for 'True Grit'
30 Parts of some wheels
31 First king of all England
32 Cordial sign-off
33 Top tube
34 Facial spots
37 See 11-Down
39 ___'acte
41 'My Name Is ___' (1965 gold album)
42 Caps
43 March on
46 1981 automotive debut
47 Power provider: Abbr.
49 Certain zest
51 Eastern pooh-bah
54 Bawl (out)
56 Ghastly
59 Capital in the Østlandet district
61 [Shiver]
63 They take 20 to 30 years to mature
65 Popular parts of platters
67 Dismissive exclamation
68 Reluctant
69 First half of an ice cream flavor
70 Like some credit cards
71 'Chase the Pig', for one
75 Shank's end
76 Pas de ___ (ballet jump)
77 Eats
78 Thomas More's Utopia, e.g.
80 Together
82 Media inits. since 1970
83 ___ End

15. Sunday: The Long and the Short of It
by Patrick Berry

Pronunciation is being butchered, and vowel play is suspected.

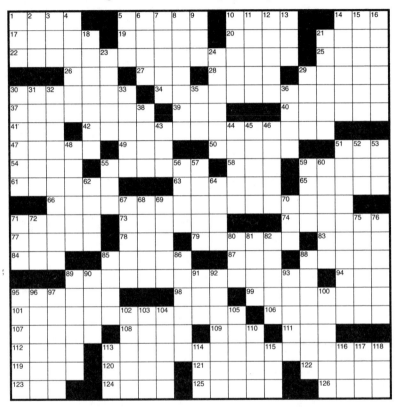

Reprinted with permission © 2013 American Crossword Puzzle Tournament.
(www.crosswordtournament.com)

ACROSS
1 Key Watergate witness
5 Bubbling over
10 World's most populous island
14 It's used for walkie-talkie transmissions
17 Card's stock
19 Knight's weapon
20 Big production
21 Academic ordeal
22 Nibbles while others are praying?
25 Roman orator
26 Bit of advice
27 Old man
28 Pod-bearing plant
29 Rudolph's master
30 Hypoallergenic fleece sources
34 Men's garment made of lathing?
37 What the Second Amendment gives one the right to do
39 Have beefs, say

40 ___ Pieces
41 Video camera button
42 Picture of a mountain decorating a bank draft?
47 Soprano's repertoire
49 Barrett of Pink Floyd
50 Character of a people
51 Savory sauce
54 Man caves
55 "I'd almost forgotten"
58 Spiteful laugh
59 Harden (to)
61 More out there, as humor
63 Auto company named after the Pleiades star cluster
65 Ideas that spread virally
66 Visible items in the painting 'Winslet Standing Fearfully on Chair'?
71 Charred
73 Relieves
74 Houston nine
77 Get together
78 Certain cage component
79 April occurrence
83 Make out
84 Ready to hit the roof
85 Trig ratios
87 Buddyroo
88 Rouse
89 Watch lousy TV shows?
94 Game akin to crazy eights
95 Work on in the editing room
98 Barley alternative, in brewing
99 Showing some growth
101 Water dogs, collectively?
106 Lovingly embraces
107 De-squeaked
108 ___ de vivre
109 Neb. neighbor
111 Corp. honcho
112 Redford's 'Havana' co-star
113 Make a sweater softer?
119 P.M. under George III
120 Twice quadri-
121 Plow man

122 Delicate headpiece
123 Bathing facility
124 Berkshire institution
125 Crime often linked to fraud
126 Quaint exclamation

DOWN

1 They play at work
2 Unimaginable time
3 Blotter abbr.
4 Bud drinker's quaff?
5 'Prince ___' ('Aladdin' song)
6 They play at work
7 At hand if needed
8 Prince of Wales's motto
9 General of the South
10 Other bad drivers, so to speak
11 Separately
12 Anglican clergyman
13 Untouched service
14 Titania and Oberon circle it
15 Oscar winner McDaniel
16 Vehicles that typically travel at 2–3 miles per hour
18 Tops of a mountain?
21 Ric of the Cars
23 Successful second ball
24 'Faust' writer
29 Blueprint detail
30 Scrape
31 Looked like a wolf
32 Fidgety alumnus?
33 Bomb's opposite
35 D.C. baseballer
36 Wraths
38 Vodka in a blue bottle
43 Millay's '___ to Silence'
44 Allen buried in Greenmount Cemetery
45 Leafy vegetable
46 Nothing to write home about
48 Eastern bloc?
51 Fossil at a Mesopotamian dig?
52 Underground treasure

53 With 86-Down, emphatic affirmative
55 Spanish gold
56 Nick and Nora's pet
57 Vietnam War copters
59 Don of morning radio
60 Lipton competitor
62 Rescue team, briefly
64 Lively party
67 Comic actress Anna
68 Kevin of 'Soapdish'
69 'Tiny Alice' playwright
70 Stick in a lock
71 Cops-and-robbers 'gunshot'
72 Thurman of 'Henry & June'
75 Performed first
76 Ecclesiastical councils
80 Choose
81 Battles
82 Cream
85 Meal served with a ladle
86 See 53-Down
88 Albatross features
89 Unlike talkies
90 ___ coffee
91 Bill, the Science Guy
92 More socially awkward
93 Party potable
95 Flies like an eagle
96 Queen Elizabeth's spouse
97 Dolores Haze's literary nickname
100 Off-track figure
102 Boot
103 'The Lone Ranger' role
104 Try to buy
105 Stupefies
110 Galba's predecessor as emperor
113 Stocking part
114 Food label info: Abbr.
115 Lowish pinochle card
116 Remind ad nauseam
117 Investment plan, for short
118 Smidgen

CHAPTER 5
HOW TO SOLVE CRYPTIC CROSSWORDS

The American composer and lyricist Stephen Sondheim is a huge fan of the cryptic crossword, being a pioneer in bringing the cryptic art to the *New York* magazine in 1968.

In that periodical, he explains:

"Mental re-punctuation is the essence of solving cryptic clues. Punctuation in ordinary writing is a guide telling the reader where and how long to pause. But the clue-writer, instead of trying to make the true meaning clear, is trying to hide it."

And that's part of the fun. We are trying to work out what the crossword creator is *really* trying to say.

I'm sure readers of this book will have all attempted a quick (or definition only) crossword before, i.e. one with simple definition clues such as 'Faithful canine (3)': Answer 'DOG'. Cryptic crosswords, however, come in around 12 different types.

We shall be looking at these clue types here, and if you've been clueless (smirk) about cryptic crosswords so far, you'll get the opportunity here to solve your first cryptic clues. They're not as hard as you might think, and they're great fun! With a little experience, you will learn to work out what type of clue you're looking for, and then solve them! While cryptic crosswords tend to be more popular in Britain than, say, the United States, I've endeavoured here to use words that will be known to you wherever you are on the crossword planet.

16. 'ANAGRAM' CLUES
Here is an example of a cryptic clue of the Anagram variety, where the solver must rearrange some letters to give the solution.

Lemon different as a fruit (5)

So how do we even begin to solve it? Well, just like a quick crossword, there is a definition. However, with a cryptic clue, there is also another part to the clue, sometimes called the wordplay.

In the wordplay there is an 'indicator', which suggests to the solver what type of clue it is. Anagram 'indicators' are words that suggest change, breaking, or that there is something wrong or unusual. So in this case, the anagram indicator is 'different' – and it is the 'lemon' that is 'different'. If you make the letters in 'lemon' different, you get the answer MELON!

A further list of Anagram indicators includes:

amiss, broken, careless, clumsy, distorted, faltering, improper, miserable, odd, peculiar, reckless, screwy, tangled, volatile and wobbly.

The indicator in a clue almost always sits alongside the letters to be rearranged to make the answer – the number of those letters should equal the letter count, marked in brackets. In our example clue, you need (5) letters. 'Lemon' is, of course, five letters long.

You are just about to solve your first cryptic crossword, in this case containing only clues of the Anagram variety.

A reminder:

1 Look for the Anagram indicator
2 Find the letters to be rearranged (and count them)
3 The rest of the clue should, by a process of elimination, be the definition.

Before you attempt to solve the puzzle itself, go through the clues underlining the Anagram indicator in each. Then put an asterisk next to the letters to be rearranged – and really, it's OK to cheat (the answers are at the back!)
I've marked up the first clue for you:

Italian city where planes* <u>diverted</u> (6)

Now solve the puzzle!

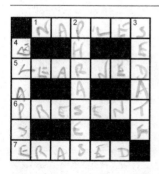

ACROSS

1 Italian city where planes diverted (6)
5 Surprisingly, a lender gained knowledge (7)
6 Gift, weird serpent (7)
7 Red Sea unfortunately wiped out (6)

DOWN

2 Sherpas struggling to produce groups of words (7)
3 Calm – when seated, flustered (6)
4 Drunk asleep, pass by (6)

17. 'HIDDEN' CLUES

So, you now have a pretty good idea how to spot anagram clues. Hidden clues, as you may have guessed, are when you can find the solution simply 'hidden' in the clue! Here's an example:

Bird kept by another one (5)

The key to solving all cryptic clues, whether of the anagram kind, hidden or any other variety, is to spot the indicator. Hidden indicators suggest concealment or being 'contained within'. In this case 'kept by' is the indicator. Note, in cryptic crosswords indicators may be phrases, not just a single word.

In the case of this clue, we are looking for a bird that is 'kept by' the letters of 'another one'. Can you see it hidden? Follow along the letters in order, and you will find your five-letter bird, anotHER ONE – HERON!

A further list of Hidden indicators includes:

amid, among, belonging to, concealed in, covered by, held by, in part, within.

So, you are just about to solve some Hidden cryptic clues.

A reminder:

1 Look for the Hidden indicator
2 Search within the letters next to the indicator for the answer.
3 The rest of the clue should, by a process of elimination, be the definition.

Here are the clues first, should you want to underline the Hidden indicator. I've done the first to give you a start.

Baby animal <u>seen in</u> musical, *Fame* (4)

Now solve the puzzle!
So, how are you doing so far? You may have thought you couldn't do cryptic crosswords, but perhaps you can after all!

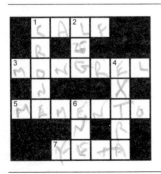

ACROSS
1 Baby animal seen in musical, *Fame* (4)
3 Mixed breed among relatives, to some extent (7)
5 Passing through Rome, men touring, finding souvenir (7)
7 Cheese swallowed by wife, tasty (4)

DOWN
1 Wrapped in Velcro, nefarious witch (5)
2 Member entering Yale, grateful (3)
4 More coming in next, rapidly (5)
6 Seventy hugs the night before! (3)

18. 'DOUBLE DEFINITION' CLUES

Did I say there is not always an indicator in a cryptic clue? No? Well there, I've said it! Double Definition clues are an exception to the rule.

Simply, there are two definitions, rather than a definition and a cryptic part to the clue. Here's an example:

Engine having a screw loose (4)

The answer's LOCO, which is both a train engine, and also suggests 'crazy', or 'having a screw loose'. Two definitions.

If you spot a clue that's relatively short, this may be a double definition clue. Perhaps it's simply a clue with just two words? Also, if you don't think you can spot any indicators suggesting your clue may be of another variety, by a process of elimination you may be looking for a Double Definition clue.

So here there's no need for me to list Double Definition indicators, as there aren't any!

Here are the clues to the next puzzle. From this puzzle onward, I'll start introducing clues of the types you have already learned. So not all of the clues in this puzzle are of the Double Definition variety. In fact, three here are of the Anagram type. Can you spot them?

ACROSS
2 Tons set off to find big hat (7)

5 Get into bed for a story (3)

6 Better hat (3)

7 Building on Mary's stonework (7)

DOWN
1 Holiday bay (6)

2 Meals distributed in Oregon's capital (5)

3 Little time for runners-up position (6)

4 Cold and brisk (5)

19. 'REVERSAL' CLUES

Here's a new type. Sometimes a cryptic crossword setter is a master of spin. There are a few words which, when read backwards, reveal another word. A personal favourite is STRESSED. In my household DESSERTS prove to be the perfect cure for anxiety!

Again, with Reversal clues, there is an indicator (which is adjacent to the letters to be reversed) to suggest something should be turned over. If the clue has been written well, it should be clear what you are to reverse, and what is the definition. Here's an example (not an easy one – most are simpler):

Plan to turn over huge cakes (9)

The Reversal indicator is 'turn over', and we are being invited to turn over MEGA-TARTS (which you could say are huge cakes!), giving you your answer: STRATAGEM!

The key to spotting a reversal clue is to find such indicators as:
back, climbing, flipping, recalled, receding, retreating, reversed, spinning, turned over, up.

Here are the clues to the next puzzle. There are four Reversal type clues. See if you can find three indicators that might suggest reversal (I've underlined the other). Do please note that, as a further trick, some Reversal indicators are specific to the 'Down' clues. Those may suggest climbing, or may simply say 'up'.

From now on, I'll let you know how many of each type of clue are present, so do take a moment finding and ringing round the indicators in these clues, where present.

The eight clues in the next puzzle are divided up as follows:

4 Reversal clues
3 Anagram clues
1 Hidden clue

Clothes with which to boast, <u>doing a twirl</u>? (4)

ACROSS
1 Clothes with which to boast, doing a twirl? (4)
5 Post a letter having used abusive language? On the contrary (7)
6 Magnate upset a shade (7)
8 Boring poet rejected (4)

DOWN
2 Caught by flea, lightweight boxer (3)
3 Swimming bather gets a little inspiration (6)
4 Prize in compartment, lifted (6)
7 Ear bashed for a specific period (3)

20. 'CONTAINER' CLUES

A Container clue is where a word is hidden inside another word – or a letter, or perhaps an anagram, is inside a word. However you look at a Container clue, it's something inside something else.

Here's an example:
  Huge deficit in fuel (8)

The answer's COLOSSAL. But can you see why? Well, it's a word meaning 'deficit' inside a word meaning 'fuel'. 'Deficit' is LOSS and 'fuel' is COAL.

But how do we know it's a Container clue? Can you spot the 'indicator'? It's simply 'in'. The word 'in' indicates structurally how the clue works. A container indicator may either suggest something is outside something, or something is inside something. When you look at these Container indicators, do start considering which suggest something is outside something else, and which suggest something is inside:

  about, boxed, captured, carrying, collected, cutting, eating, entertaining, feeding, in, held by, locked up, outside, swallowed by, welcoming, within.

In the next puzzle, there are four Container clues. I have underlined the Container indicator in one of those clues. Can you spot the rest? Just to give you a further clue, three of the four Container clues lead you to a solution comprised of a word within a word, but in another clue it is a letter inside a word. If I were to tell you that sometimes in cryptic crosswords we use words to indicate letters – we shall look at this in more detail later – do try to consider which words might suggest the letter O, which looks like a zero.

As I say, coming up are the clues. Don't try to solve them yet, just look for indicators. There are:

4 Container clues
2 Hidden clues
1 Double Definition clue
1 Anagram clue

Little movement <u>involving</u> newspaper – that's very sad (6)

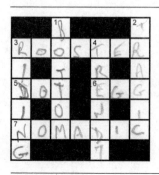

ACROSS
3 Nothing in duty list for early riser (7)
5 Some mud, otherwise a little speck (3)
6 Encourage to find something for breakfast (3)
7 Mad icon randomly roaming about (7)

DOWN
1 Lowest point being taken by robot to master (6)
2 Little movement involving newspaper – that's very sad (6)
3 Terrible noise in apparatus on a bicycle, perhaps? (6)
4 Attempt to conceal rear, being fashionable (6)

21. 'SOUND-ALIKE' CLUES

This is where the answer sounds like another word, which is indicated in the clue by a Sound-alike indicator. Here's an example:

Cold country, we hear (6)

'We hear' is a very common Sound-alike indicator. In this case we are looking for a word meaning 'cold' that sounds like a word meaning 'country'. Note that the indicator should be next to the word that sounds like the answer, *not* adjacent to the definition. The answer is CHILLY, which sounds like CHILE.

Sound-alike clues seem to provoke many solvers into venting their spleen online. After all, the pronunciation of a word in Tennessee, Glasgow and Mumbai might vary considerably.

Here are some more Sound-alike indicators:
aloud, broadcast, it's said, on the radio, pronounced, reported, say.

Here are the clues to the next puzzle, in which there are:

4 Sound-alike clues
2 Anagram clues
1 Hidden clue
1 Double Definition clue

Remember to ring round the indicators where they're present.

And now solve the puzzle!

ACROSS
1 Cut of meat, bet it's pronounced? (5)
5 Sweet found in this? Eminem, we hear (7)
6 Loan may put right something irregular (7)
8 Begin to jump (5)

DOWN
2 Sovereign's seat hurled, it's said? (6)
3 Unusual map showing electrical unit (3)
4 Sounds like tradesman's in the basement! (6)
7 Found in bedroom, a Turkish rug (3)

22. 'DELETIONS'

In these clues, something has been taken away. Here's an example:

Begin shortly to find film idol (4)

Words like 'shortly' may suggest a word has been shortened in length. In this case, a word meaning 'begin' is seen 'shortly'. START becomes STAR, the film idol. Deletions may happen anywhere in the word, so perhaps the first letter will disappear, or the last, or the central letter. 'Headless' might suggest the first letter, or 'head' of the word is deleted. 'Heartless' may suggest the middle has gone. 'Endless', and we have lost the last letter.

Other Deletion indicators include:

abridged, cut, gutted, losing capital, losing the lead, skimmed, tailless.

Here we have:

3 Deletion clues
2 Anagram clues
1 Hidden clue
1 Sound-alike clue

And here's the puzzle:

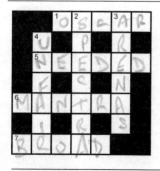

ACROSS

1 Statuette wrapped in Pacino's cardigan (5)

5 Required to be worked like dough, say? (6)

6 Catcher's endless secret incantation (6)

7 American girl in another country, though not initially (5)

DOWN

2 Bands of colours in woven carpets (7)

3 Stadia as near development (6)

4 Topless place of entertainment, immoral (6)

23. 'CRYPTIC DEFINITION' CLUES – OR PUNS

Cryptic Definition clues usually end with a question mark. There isn't a definition part and a cryptic part, as in most crossword clues, but simply a swerving play on words, where a little lateral thought is required.

Jammed cylinder? (5,4) isn't actually the reason why my car doesn't seem to want to start every morning. Instead we are searching for a cylinder full of jam, or a SWISS ROLL. Another example might be:

A stiff examination (4,6)

I hope this whole solving experience has stretched that grey matter to the full, but you'd have to be going flat out to need a POST MORTEM, the examination of a stiff!

Because of the nature of a Cryptic Definition clue, the only real indicator is the question mark at its conclusion; though do be aware that a question mark doesn't guarantee a Cryptic Definition clue. We setters sometimes use the mark to suggest there is some extra devious wordplay going on in the clue, Cryptic Definition or not!

See if you can ring round the indicators, where relevant, in the clues for the next puzzle. There are:

3 Cryptic Definition clues
3 Anagram clues
2 Deletion clues
1 Hidden clue
1 Double Definition clue

Now solve the puzzle!

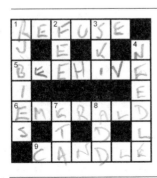

ACROSS

1 Don't accept rubbish (6)
5 Comb in this hairstyle? (7)
6 Red, male turning a shade of green (7)
9 Something wicked? (6)

DOWN

1 Carelessly buries gems (6)
2 Eat endlessly for a payment (3)
3 Almost slide out of control, and go downhill (3)
4 Playing record, might one get into the groove? (6)
7 Inside packet, Athenian letter from Greece (3)
8 Tot or dad, confused (3)

24. 'CHARADE' CLUES

Perhaps you've played the party game of charades. It's where someone describes a word, perhaps a book or a film, by acting out each part of the word or words, in turn. Some words were seemingly coined just for a Charade clue! 'Sunglasses' can be divided into SUNG and LASSES. 'Carpenter' is CARP and ENTER. In Charade clues there is a definition, as usual, and then in turn, each part of the clue is also defined. Here's an example:

Flamboyant style made God hurt (7)

'God' in this case is PAN and 'Hurt' is ACHE, for the definition 'Flamboyant style'.

You may have noted, indicators aren't present in this sort of clue either.

In the clues that follow, there are:

5 Charade clues
1 Hidden clue
1 Anagram clue
1 Reversal clue

And here's the puzzle:

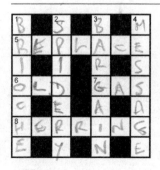

ACROSS

5 Substitute for salesman, delicate fabric (7)

6 Ancient part of Moldova (3)

7 Hang back for oxygen, perhaps? (3)

8 Fish for something on the bride's finger? (7)

DOWN

1 Soft roll with spirit, Mr Guevara? (7)

2 Thin and spindly, dry pies ruined (7)

3 Something cheap made drinking establishment profit (7)

4 Chaos, then time for communication (7)

25. 'ABBREVIATION' CLUES

This is the bit where it's useful to consider which words might suggest initials or abbreviations.

The word 'Elephant' in a clue wouldn't suggest any initials, as we wouldn't in everyday life see 'E' and think ELEPHANT. However, if we see 'P' on a road sign, we might think PARKING. This is where things get ever so slightly British. Frankly, not everyone plays cricket. However, the words 'Caught', 'Bowled' or 'Wicket' would, with a little practice, lead us to c, b and w respectively. And why would Americans, for example (although a few play cricket), be expected not to get stumped (excuse the pun, if it makes sense to you!) by cricket terminology?

Here are a few words that may suggest abbreviations. I've listed one word per letter here, but there are several possibilities for each letter. There are many two-letter indicators too. For example, 'church' may lead you to CH, and 'street' to ST.

article – A, *black* – B, *cold* – C, *democrat* – D, *drug (Ecstasy)* – E,
Fahrenheit – F, *good* – G, *hosptial* – H, *one (Roman numerals)* – I, *joker* – J,
king – K, *left* – L, *motorway* – M, *name* – N, *oxygen* – O, *page* – P, *queen* – Q,
river – R, *seconds* – S, *time* – T, *universal* – U, *very* – V, *west*– W, *kiss*– X,
year – Y, *zulu* – Z.

Furthermore, the word 'initially' may suggest you are to look for the initial letter of the adjacent word. Ideas such as 'end of' may suggest you are to look for the last letter of the next word.

The next puzzle contains:

4 Abbreviation clues
2 Hidden clues
1 Anagram clue
1 Charade clue

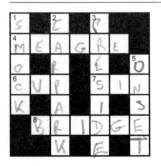

ACROSS

4 Lean into some agreement (6)

6 Cowboys initially raised trophy (3)

7 In churches I never do wrong (3)

8 Golden Gate has one black edge (6)

DOWN

1 Last of furs, fake coat-like garment (5)

2 Where vehicles are left with fish on ship (3,4)

3 Exercise authority, making first of prisoners live (7)

5 Start breaking stone (5)

26. '&LIT' CLUES

& Lit simply means 'and literally there's the answer'. There is just the wordplay, and (arguably!) no further need for a definition. Here's an example:

No fellow for mixing (4,4)

'For mixing' might suggest that the other letters need jumbling up, as an anagram. And there are eight letters in 'no fellow'.
The answer is LONE WOLF. But where's the definition?

Well, the whole clue is the definition: a lone wolf is certainly 'no fellow for mixing'!

&Lit clues are rare beasts indeed, and considered the Holy Grail of crossword setting, as they're elusive, and often difficult to create. Having said that, they can be the most beautiful and elegant of things.

Here are the clues to the next puzzle, in which there are:

3 &Lit clues
2 Hidden clues
1 Anagram clue
1 Abbreviation clue
1 Double Definition clue

And here's the puzzle:

ACROSS
1 I'm a leader of Muslims! (4)
4 Cops all cooked seafood (7)
6 Enraged, possibly? (7)
7 Good antique, shiny and yellow (4)

DOWN
2 Discovered in Palermo, large tooth (5)
3 Sulked, seeing vehicle (5)
4 Some discourteous language (5)
5 Seen in gang, elegant heavenly being (5)

So now you have tried just about every possible type of clue, though many clues combine more than one cryptic device. Where do you go next?

Personally, I'd recommend Everyman in the *Observer*, Monday's *Guardian* (usually by Rufus), and also the *Guardian* online Quiptic puzzles, an example of which you will soon meet. The *Daily Telegraph* too is good for beginners.

I've also been running a 'How To Solve' guide in the magazine *Q Crossword Mix*, published by Puzzler Media Ltd.

If you're not sure how a particular solution has been reached, try:

• www.fifteensquared.net, where the *Guardian*, the *Independent* and the *Financial Times* crosswords are explained and discussed, daily.

• www.bigdave44.com, for the *Daily Telegraph* cryptic.

• www.times-xwd-timeslivejournal.com, for *The Times*, but don't be put off here by many of the bloggers who often post their (often remarkably quick) times for solving the puzzle!

Great references for learning to solve include Don Manley's *Chambers Crossword Manual* and Tim Moorey's *How To Master The Times Crossword*.

And tell your friends how much fun this is, too! I do hope, like me, you've caught the cryptic bug! Enjoy!

.

CHAPTER 6
OTHER TYPES OF CROSSWORD

Standard definition-based crosswords, or those with cryptic clues, are just two of a wide range of puzzles. Across the world, puzzle fans have become used to their preferred crossword, often quick or cryptic.

Occasionally, though, a newspaper will branch out and publish something different from the norm. There are plenty of specialist puzzle magazines on the market nowadays. Puzzle fans can buy a whole book of diagramless puzzles, for example. The following are some examples of crosswords in various forms.

QUIPTIC

A 'web-only cryptic puzzle for beginners and those in a hurry' was introduced to the *Guardian* website in 1999. At that time there was no real online crossword community as there is today, so it was difficult for would-be cryptic solvers to get started if they didn't have a tame cruciverbalist to hand. *Guardian* crossword editor Hugh Stephenson came up with the idea of a weekly 'easy' cryptic which "would embolden aspirants teetering at the end of the diving board almost ready to take the plunge, and help to teach them some crossword basics along the way". The Quiptic remit was, essentially 'Keep it simple', but Hugh also wanted the puzzle to have a proper *Guardian* flavour, including references to left-of-centre politics and social concerns.

27. *Guardian* Quiptic
By Orlando

ACROSS

1 Flower, say, in black container (9)

6 Extra snake almost died (5)

9 Be pleased with those who applaud quickly (4,3,8)

10 An insect used to be quiet (4)

11 Initially *Evening Standard* journalists love coffee (8)

14 Something one has to have when pro is in a mess? (9)

15 Wrong end of Dundee cake (5)

16 Giant bird a non-starter (5)

18 Garfunkel recording that's seen in gallery? (4,2,3)

20 I mention sound or vision (8)

21 Walk with difficulty, having wilted? (4)

25 New boots lift chap up – they're made for walking! (6,9)

26 Subject of article by Orlando (5)

27 Where university education may lead? Not entirely (2,1,6)

DOWN

1 Feel miserable when not on deck? (5)

2 Provides accommodation for kids (5,2)

3 Makes 'ot grub (4)

4 Ship's company sounded cocky? (4)

5 Very different – like those in Cracow and those in Gdansk? (5,5)

6 Cherished desire possibly revealed to Parisian (10)

7 One putting clothes on kitchen sideboard (7)

8 Gorgeous creature taking one's temperature is deceptive (9)

12 Having an object, I have to follow Ford van (10)

13 Jack Sprat wouldn't talk (4,3,3)

14 Photo sent out immediately (2,3,4)

17 Quaver from end of anthem held by singer (7)

19 Airman coming from Scandinavia to Russia (7)

22 Thrash tense European (5)

23 Firm American lawyer closing bars (4)

24 Part of church any parishioners should examine at first (4)

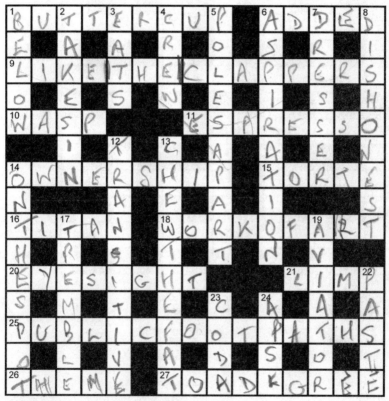

First published in the *Guardian* newspaper.

28. Anagrams

Unscramble the clues to find the one-word solutions.

(crossword grid)

ACROSS
8 SODA PIE
9 CANOE
10 AS CRUEL
11 TREES
12 PEACH
14 RAT SUET
16 LET CARP
18 ROLES
20 ELGAR
22 SIMPERS
24 THING
25 DELTAIC

DOWN
1 SCRAPE
2 SECRET ID
3 FILO
4 BRIDES
5 OF ISRAEL
6 LEFT
7 RUE NUT
13 NEAT TIPS
15 STAY NUDE
16 PLY SON
17 ACE PIE
19 RESULT
21 GEAR
23 PEST

29. Link words

Every solution may either be placed immediately before, or immediately after the three words in the clue to form well-known words or phrases, For example, the clue 'SPIDER, WRENCH, BUSINESS (6) would yield the answer MONKEY (SPIDER MONKEY, MONKEY WRENCH, MONKEY BUSINESS).

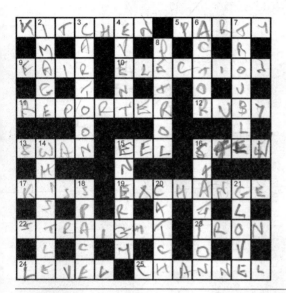

ACROSS

1 GARDEN, ROLL, SOUP (7)
5 POOPER, SLUMBER, WORKING (5)
9 FUN, GAME, GROUND (4)
10 DAY, GENERAL, LOCAL (8)
11 CUB, ROVING, SPORTS (8)
12 LIPS, RING, TUESDAY (4)
13 MUTE, NECK, SONG (4)
15 CONGER, ELECTRIC, SAND (3)
16 FISH, IRISH, PAN (4)
17 CHASE, CURL, FRENCH (4)
19 BLOWS, RATE, STOCK (8)
22 DEAD, HOME, TALKING (8)
23 CURTAIN, MAIDEN, STEAM (4)
24 BEST, GROUND, SPIRIT (5)
25 ENGLISH, NEWS, TELEVISION (7)

DOWN

2 CONSCIOUS, PUBLIC, SPITTING (5)
3 ANIMATED, CHARACTER, STRIP (7)
4 FIELD, HAPPY, HORIZON (5)
6 CHARACTER, CHILD, HAM (5)
7 DOUBLE, MAKER, SPOT (7)
8 BOMB, DRIVEN, PUMP (6)
14 DIXIE, DOG, TIN (7)
15 DARK, NUCLEAR, SOLAR (6)
16 RADIO, WAGON, WEATHER (7)
18 BREATHING, CADET, PROBE (5)
20 COLD, SAFETY, WINDOW (5)
21 BASEBALL, BOXING, PUPPET (5)

30. Sixer

Every solution begins with one of six letters. Rearrange these to find, according to Wikipedia, America's 34th most populous city. That city's name can also be rearranged to form another word.

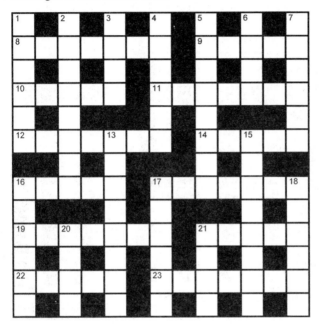

ACROSS

8 Couple (7)

9 Scottish person of rank, chief of a clan (5)

10 Plant used to make rope (5)

11 Messy (7)

12 Italian liqueur (7)

14 Item on Meryl Streep's mantelpiece? (5)

16 Top of the milk (5)

17 Maritime disaster – box office success (7)

19 Great Lake (7)

21 Hardy type of wheat (5)

22 Censure – fine-grained rock (5)

23 Renault (anag) – impartial (7)

DOWN

1 State of equilibrium (6)

2 Clear soup (8)

3 Implement (4)

4 Interstellar cloud of gas and dust (6)

5 Act of police surveillance (8)

6 Peaceful (4)

7 Drink of the gods (6)

13 Appealing to high-income consumers (8)

15 Southern hemisphere capital city (8)

16 Particular (6)

17 Difficult (and spiky?) (6)

18 Cows (6)

20 Amphibian – scoundrel (4)

21 Bullet – shot of liquor – garden pest (4)

31. Thematic Puzzles

Nowadays it's possible to produce thematic crosswords, via crossword software, at the flick of a few switches. The clues usually have to be manually written, but this puzzle was produced from the Crossword Compiler database, which includes various thematic lists, and various grid shapes.

I chose the shape of a camera and a film list to produce this one.

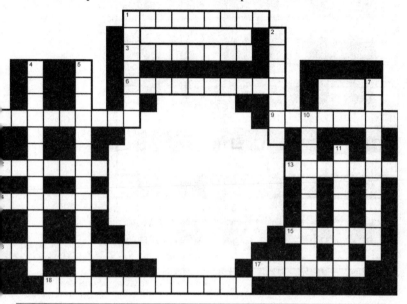

ACROSS

1 Actor – big lemons (anag) (3,6)
3 Actor who played Parcher in *A Beautiful Mind* (2,6)
6 *Gattaca* actor (5,5)
8 Star of *Midnight Cowboy* (3,6)
9 *Scarface* actor (2,6)
12 US actor and pro-wrestler (3,4)
13 Star of *When Harry Met Sally* (3,4)
14 Actor in *St Elmo's Fire* and *Wayne's World* (3,4)
15 Taiwanese-born US film director (3,3)
16 Ali in *Ali* (4,5)
17 *Saturday Night Live* comedienne and author of *Bossypants* (4,3)
18 *The Misfits* star (7,6)

DOWN

1 Star of *She Done Him Wrong* and *I'm No Angel* (3,4)
2 Alfie in *Alfie* (4,3)
4 Alex in *Flashdance* (8,5)
5 A friend of *Friends* (5,9)
7 Star of *Beetlejuice* and *Edward Scissorhands* (6,5)
10 *Easy Rider* star, with Dennis Hopper and Jack Nicholson (5,5)
11 Chinese-American martial artist and film star (5,3)

32. General Knowledge

(Self-explanatory, really.)

ACROSS

8 US author and philosopher who said "It's not what you look at that matters, it's what you see" (7)

9 Hugh Laurie medical drama (5)

10 Cloth worn as a sarong, etc, in India (5)

11 Protective railing along the edge of a roof (7)

12 *Sing as We Go* singer of WWII (6,6)

15 Medieval allegory by Boccaccio (3,9)

19 European mammal of the weasel family with blackish fur (7)

20 Athenian politician whose code was unpopular for its severity (5)

22 Lord or sovereign to whom allegiance is due, according to feudal law (5)

23 Bob Marley hit on the *Exodus* album (3,4)

DOWN

1 Study of the ear (7)

2 Zen Buddhist riddle such as "What is the sound of one hand clapping?" (4)

3 Italian noble family producing three popes (6)

4 Process of making an urban area attractive to young moneyed consumers (13)

5 Tom ___, satirical author known for his *Wilt* series (6)

6 Another name for a spittoon (8)

7 Australian city that hosted the 1962 Commonwealth Games (5)

13 Great warrior of Homer's *Iliad* (8)

14 Toronto feature completed in 1976 when it was the world's tallest free-standing structure (2,5)

16 Carol ___, lead singer of the 1980s band T'Pau (6)

17 Drama starring Jon Hamm as New York ad executive Don Draper (3,3)

18 The Beatles' fruity record label? (5)

21 River flowing through Bristol, England (4)

33. Crossword Puzzle

Crosswords need not be in a grid form that is of American or British style. The simplest way of piecing words together is pretty much like this, but of course with so few cross-checked letters, the setter should aim to ease up on the clues a bit.

Here's a Cross-word Puzzle. I was considering having every clue simply read 'Cross', but I thought that might leave some solvers feeling – how can I put it – cross?

ACROSS

3 Cross (5)
5 Cross (12)
6 Cross – card game (6)
11 Cross (9)
12 Cross – Disney dwarf (6)
13 Cross – like a crustacean? (6)
15 Cross (6)

DOWN

1 Cross (8)
2 Cross – hand width (4)
4 Cross – US car (4)
7 Cross (9)
8 Cross (7)
9 Cross – serve rat (anag) (8)
10 Cross – like an insect? (7)
14 Cross – word for 'entrance' written upwards (4)

34. Community Puzzle (Liverpool)

Cryptic clues are in bold

ACROSS

1 **Ordinary person – but no woman then?** (8)

6 Airs and ___, (three buildings on Liverpool's Pier Head) (6)

9 John ___, poet (1631-1700) (6)

10 **Irish emblem to imitate about right, alongside Knotty Ash** (8)

11 Door post (4)

13 **Loosely used cross-word for Liverpudlians** (8)

15 **No lemon? That's fair enough** (7)

17 Write a crossword (7)

19 Deep valleys (7)

20 **Trounce the French band from Liverpool** (7)

22 John Lennon's advice, as opposed to going to war (4,4)

25 Bigfoot (4)

27 Describing furniture to be assembled by the buyer (4-4)

28 Employ (4,2)

30 **French say thanks for river in Liverpool** (6)

31 Tollgate (8)

DOWN

2 Describing native language e.g. spoken by 13 across (10)

3 **Anfield colour in azure, dyed** (3)

4 **Everton sweets sound like ground meat** (5)

5 Person who didn't arrive at the party (2-4)

6 **Liverpool statesman disappeared to collect young man on the street** (9)

7 Clothes horse (5)

8 Engrave (4)

12 Sarnie (5)

14 **Block trade that's dodgy where ships' cargo loaded** (6,4)

16 Crossword celebration of a 100 years (9)

18 Mad as a box of frogs (5)

21 **Music genre and French Rainhill locomotive** (6)

23 Female singers (5)

24 Go in (5)

26 **European Union with pound going up – and down!** (4)

29 Liverpool stand (3)

Across
1. EVERYMAN
6. GRACES
9. DRYDEN
10. SHAMROCK
11. JAMB
13. SCOUSERS
15. JUSTICE
17. COMPILE
19. CANYONS
20. BEATLES
22. MAKE LOVE
25. YETI
27. FLATPACK
28. TAKE ON
30. MERSEY
31. TURNPIKE

COMMUNITY PUZZLE

In February 2013 I travelled round Britain on a seven-stop tour, meeting some fabulous crossword-loving communities, and at each location creating a puzzle with that community concerned with the things they love about their own city/ county. Local newspapers were brilliant, often publishing the puzzle, and providing the crossword with some wonderful publicity.

The aim of the tour was to bring communities together, to get people excited about words, and to have a whole barrel of fun at the same time.

One such stop had to be Liverpool, the birthplace of one Arthur Wynne.

On the preceding pages is the puzzle we created together, which was published in Liverpool's *Echo*.

(The story of the tour, which visited Brighton, Bristol, Poole, Oxford, Shrewsbury, Liverpool, Manchester and London, can be read at www.crosswordcentenary.com.)

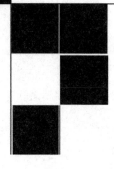

SECTION 3
CROSSWORD PEOPLE: SETTERS AND THEIR THINKING, CHAMPION SOLVERS, AND EDITORS

CHAPTER 7
THE SETTERS/CONSTRUCTORS

"So ... what do you do for a living?"

It's a pretty standard opener at a party, and the reply "I'm a crossword setter" is met with one of a number of responses:

"I guess someone has to do that" is a personal un-favourite.

"Oooh, you must be really clever" is another. At which point I am just grateful these people haven't witnessed my hapless attempts to fold a shirt, or to wire a plug. And while many of my colleagues have postgraduate doctorates, I trail in some way behind with a third-class degree in Maths and Music. However, what helps to further cement the perception that if I write crosswords I must therefore be brainy, is my appearance.

I am balding, and I wear glasses.

Another very common response is the blank, slowly computing, countenance. Might they not have quite heard right, or perhaps they simply didn't know what a crossword was, and were afraid to ask? A guy at my local gym, with whom I had chatted off and on for at least two years, recently introduced me to another club member as a cartoonist.

Personally, I find getting to know crossword writers brings a whole new understanding to solving their puzzles. Conversely, if I am familiar with the puzzles of a particular name or pseudonym, I am rarely surprised by the human behind the puzzle when meeting them. After all, how much more intimately can we get to know someone? Surely there is no more profound relationship than that between setter and solver.

So let's unmask some of the greatest wordplayers in the world, beginning with:

JOHN GRIMSHAW
John Grimshaw Shaw isn't Grim. He's a likeable and brilliant raconteur, and, like most of us, painfully obsessed with crosswords.

The first *Times2* appeared on November 1, 1993, with a fanfare of publicity including an article by Philip Howard. It was the brainchild of Richard Browne, who set every one for the next nine years until taking up his present position as cryptic crossword editor in 2002, handing over the reins of the *Times2* to John Grimshaw, who is solely responsible for the puzzle.

I can thoroughly recommend the *Times2*, as it has that extra layer of ingenuity, created in such a way that even if you don't spot it, you are still left with an enjoyable solve.

Here John talks us through his thinking behind the puzzle:

"However many grids I've filled – and my total of *Times2* daily and jumbo puzzles now stands at over 3,500 – there is always that moment of blank thought that occurs when looking at the next grid to fill. Putting in that first word is always something of a psychological hurdle – why choose this one, why that? For that reason, I've always liked to constrain my possibilities a bit before starting. It seems paradoxical, but limiting oneself in this way does seem to stimulate creativity, as Schoenberg discovered through his 12-tone system.

"So I now nearly always start by seeding the grid with a small theme, which immediately either fixes some letters or limits choices at each stage. It might simply be that I put the letter 'D' in every cell (square) on the main diagonal, or decide that four symmetrically arranged entries should all be genres of music. This ploy has a double advantage, as it gets me past that intimidating first step but also later provides a potential point of interest for the solver if they spot what I've done. In this way I like to think I keep myself fresh, since every puzzle sets me a slightly different challenge."

On the next page you can attempt a puzzle chosen by John, and published in 2006, which forms part of a 92-puzzle series. It's based on British film director Peter Greenaway's *Tulse Luper Suitcases* project, a complex multimedia undertaking initially intended to be made up of three 'source' films and one feature film, a 16-episode TV series and 92 DVDs.

John says, "I set out to create a series of 92 puzzles each loosely based on the contents of one of Greenaway's 92 different 'suitcases'. This puzzle was for suitcase 52, which contains 55 paintings of men on horseback, so the thematic nature of six entries is easily understood. What solvers wouldn't have spotted is that the number 55 is also reflected in the puzzle – but you might have to do some clue-number addition to confirm that.

"Perhaps I've created a rod for my own back in incorporating such themes, some of which do involve a bit of extra work on my part, but I do firmly believe that setters should put their fair share of effort in to match that of their solvers, and perhaps this particular puzzle exemplifies that more than any of my other T2s."

35. *Times2* Crossword
by John Grimshaw, 2006

ACROSS

1 Person on horseback (10)
7 Haul up (5)
8 Rider in contests (7)
10 Fish eggs (3)
11 State of excess fat (9)
13 Science of vision (6)
14 Watch with hinged cover (6)
17 Gum trees (9)
19 Frozen water (3)
20 Islam holy month (7)
22 Caper, grotesque (*arch.*) (5)
23 One riding coach horse (10)

DOWN

1 Respected; distinguished (7)
2 Not characteristic (9)
3 Horses (6)
4 Bitterly regret (3)
5 __ Shaw, US jazz clarinettist and bandleader (5)
6 Driver of horse-drawn fighting vehicle (10)
9 Revival (in popularity) (10)
12 Bellini opera with English Civil War setting (1,8)
15 Lover of Isolde (7)
16 Glassy mineral (6)
18 Jewellery item with carved portrait (5)
21 Small round mark (3)

By kind permission of *The Times*.

36. *Guardian* 'Quick' Crossword
by Michael Curl

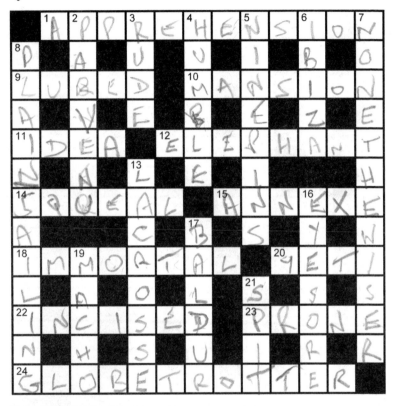

First published in the *Guardian* newspaper.

MICHAEL CURL

Quick crossword setter for the *Guardian*, Michael Curl says he "enjoyed a misspent youth in an awkward age – born too late to be a beatnik, too early to be a hippy." As a former computer programmer, Michael surely qualifies as stereotypical fodder for a crossword setter.

ACROSS

1 Trepidation (12)
9 Enticed (5)
10 Large house (7)
11 Notion (4)
12 Large pachyderm (8)
14 Equals (anag) (6)
15 Extension to a building (6)
18 Deathless (8)
20 Abominable snowman (4)
22 Engraved (7)
23 Lying face downwards (5)
24 One who travels widely (12)

DOWN

2 Arriviste (7)
3 Uncivil (4)
4 Lowly (6)
5 Skittles (8)
6 One of the Balearic Islands (5)
7 Knowing no more than before (4,3,5)
8 Easy progress (5,7)
13 Sport with sticks (8)
16 Blot on the landscape (7)
17 Son of Odin – with less on top? (6)
19 Exaggeratedly masculine (5)
21 Narrow peninsula – Polish companion? (4)

"It might be argued that quick crosswords are to cryptic crosswords what pie and chips are to a gourmet meal," he says. "But there's nowt wrong with pie and chips and many people prefer it."

At a rough estimate, around three times more people in Britain tackle the quick crossword, as opposed to the cryptic – although the latter figure is fast catching up.

Curl also sets excellent and entertaining 'entry level' cryptic crosswords for the *Guardian* as Orlando (a pseudonym that is based on his middle name Roland).

"The quick crossword does offer the setter considerably less scope for cleverness. But one can try to spice things up occasionally with the odd double definition where the two parts seem incongruous (like the old chestnut 'Split – unite (6)' for CLEAVE), with the occasional quirky (but fair) general knowledge clue, and an anagram clue or two."

Note from the author: here is an opportunity for me to apologize for an incident at his Leeds home circa 1995. I was a rookie espresso drinker, had never dabbled in sophisticated coffee before, or drunk from those dainty and impractical espresso cups with tiny handles … Yes, I know, Michael, I still owe you a mahogany dining table.

DAVID ASTLE

In 2010 David Astle, an Australian setter, was selected to co-host *Letters and Numbers* on national TV, fulfilling the role of dictionary oracle, much as Susie Dent does on the *Countdown* equivalent in the UK.

Currently, with the show in hiatus, he has continued to create puzzles, a weekly language column, plus three titles for word-lovers, including the crossword memoir *Puzzled* and *Cluetopia*.

Fame certainly has its delightfully quirky moments, as David explains:

"One side effect of the telly job is being recognized in the street, not always a healthy prospect for a cryptic crossword maker. Walking my dog one morning, just after dawn, I came across a council worker operating a STOP/SLOW sign beside some road works.

"Barely light, the man warned me about the pots in the oncoming footpath. I thanked him and kept walking, a little confused by his remark. The pots? Surely he meant potholes? And that's when the penny dropped.

"I wheeled back and pointed to his STOP sign, saying 'POST'. And he responded 'SPOT'. And I returned with 'OPTS'. And he laughed and said, 'TOPS'. We shook hands. Gordon was a puzzle-nut and lover of the game show. Though perhaps I went too far when telling him his name was an anagram of 'DRONGO'."

David explains a little about the crossword community in Australia:

"Once upon a time a crossword setter only had an inkling of how his or her solvers may respond to a clue. Not now – the fibre-optic cables buzz with feedback.

"Locally here, the main puzzle outlet is the Fairfax group of papers, namely the *Sydney Morning Herald* and the *Age* in Melbourne. Sister papers, the two run a stable of seven compilers in sync. As aliases, the clue-mongers are known by their initials. I'm DA, which stands for Don't Attempt, or Dangerously Addictive, depending on your inclination.

"My colleagues are DS (David Sutton), DH (Donald Harrison), RM (Rose McGinley), NS (Nancy Sibtain), DP (David Plomley) and newcomer LR (Liam Runnalls). Another setter of note is David Stickley, better known as Styx in the *Financial Times*, who creates the Stickler crossword for the *Daily Telegraph*, while 2011 sadly marked the passing of the beloved pioneer Shirl O'Brien, the elegant Auster of *Guardian* fame.

"I feel like my preoccupation has become my occupation. I've always been hooked on letters, an addict of the alphabet, a jumble junkie. Thank God there was an outlet like clue-writing, otherwise I may have ended up on a park bench, swapping syllables with pigeons.

"The man to grant me a break was Lindsey Browne, alias LB, the giant of Australian crosswords. A fixture at the *Sydney Morning Herald*, LB reigned the popular imagination for over 50 years. I sent him ingénue clues through the mail. Handwritten grids. Clunky anagrams. Somehow he tolerated my undergrad humour, refining my clues with good grace and sharp wit.

"My *Herald* debut came in 1983. I was 21, fresh out of university. August 6 – I still remember the buzz of seeing my puzzle in print. To my shame I stalked the morning trains to see how solvers were responding. You'll be glad to learn I drew the line at giving them bonus hints."

Here are a few of David's favourite clues:

1 Cougar's kinky date – unclothed to make things more appealing (5-4)
2 Web novel? He penned it! (2,5)
3 Drifting item belongs at sea! (7,2,1,6)
4 Contrary sources describe old admirer's position (5,4)
5 Privates dope Florentine shrinks (9)
6 Me: cats or dogs and so on with rightful human risk? I warn otherwise!
(2,6,3,4,6,3,6,2,4,9)

BRIAN GREER

Brian Greer, formerly of Strabane, Ireland is now resident in Portland, Oregon.

Greer, who writes cryptic crosswords for *The Times*, the *Guardian* (as 'Brendan', an Irishman who went to America) and the *Independent* (as Virgilius), explains the latter nom de guerre:

"Virgilius was an Irish monk who worked on manuscripts and composed acrostics while doing so. I now somewhat regret making such a pretentious choice."

But Greer's crosswords are pretension-free. He is arguably the master of the cryptic theme and, as a resident of the US, seems to have combined the excellent constructor mentality of American puzzle makers with the British love of a great body swerve. His themes are accessible. Furthermore, he has mastered the art of writing thematically while ensuring the solver rarely needs to resort to the dictionary or the Internet.

Personally, I believe the amount of time spent solving a puzzle must always be exceeded by the amount of fun taken from so doing. And Brian seems to agree, for his puzzles don't take hours, but leave the solver feeling satisfied, and clever. After all, who likes to be defeated morning after morning?

Brian describes his routine, and his crossword mindset:

"I get up much earlier than I did in my youth, often to feed the cat, and to make a concoction of lime juice, touch of cayenne, honey and boiling water. My wife and I, if we can, then walk a couple of miles to a favourite café for coffee.

"Themes come to me at odd times, and part of my mind is on watch for them whatever I'm doing. Grid-filling is done step-by-step and with a lot of patience, via Crossword Compiler software.

(continued on page 92)

37. Stryptic Puzzle
From the *Sydney Morning Herald* by David Astle

Use either straight or cryptic clues. You get to choose which to tackle.

Reprinted with kind permission of David Astle.

STRAIGHT CLUES

ACROSS

1 Train that stops at all stations; wide-ranging outfielder (7)
5 Berserk (7)
9 Punishes comprehensively (6,3,4,2)
10 Introduce (5,2)
11 One providing meanings (7)
12 On the beach (6)
13 Musician manipulating a chanter (8)
16 Hemlock reverser (8)
17 Lower in rank (6)
20 Advance screening (7)
22 Beginning (4-3)
23 Iridescent parrot (7,8)
24 Thickset (7)
25 Diffusion of fluids through a membrane (7)

DOWN

1 Former Japanese province – or loose-rinded fruit (7)
2 Devastating (5-10)
3 Network of cables distributing electricity (5,4)
4 Chubby (6)
5 Relating to a celebrated Austrian psychoanalyst (8)
6 Socially distant (5)
7 Exercise zero clemency (4,2,9)
8 Party's food supplier (7)
14 Theory embracing multiple ideologies (9)
15 Illicit passenger in hiding (8)
16 Tablet offering headache relief (7)
18 Disproves (7)
19 Brightly coloured (6)
21 Infuse (5)

CRYPTIC CLUES

ACROSS

1 Twitter link remains integral to regular chat range (7)
5 Cross borne among relatives (7)
9 Dummy coated tinted cane woven in Woodwork (7,3,5)
10 Substitute materials (7)
11 Keen collector initially keeping eggs from seal (7)
12 More likely to come into this world with setter and pauper? (6)
13 Opts for affected meat prior to exercise (4,2,2)
16 Polish honoured leader escaping hit (8)
17 Possibly prepare cuppa, cupping very odd cuppa alternative (6)
20 Grant a way for rides on show (3,4)
22 Heretic ridiculed if Nicene extract backfired (7)
23 She oversees lots of beer during holiday, escorting a drink chap (4,6,5)
24 Wrap-around skirt I displayed in arty scene (7)
25 Old ship with holes in it? (7)

DOWN

1 Some rhymes are dull? (7)
2 Worked in the S&M game, down at heel? (8,3,4)
3 Asian superb with flags occupying tense borders (9)
4 My endless love for oldie (6)
5 It's valuable to nuke now and then in atomic conflict (4,4)
6 Like a praline off your trolley? (5)
7 Overrated manor's pitch? (10,5)
8 Paparazzo's hood, perhaps, sees Poles caught during spring (4,3)
14 New folks with a kink have no chance Down Under (9)
15 Feud nearly opening one short on tape (8)
16 Second problem a comfort (4,3)
18 Record next rookie at the wheel (1-6)
19 Break in US/Thai strife (6)
21 Crack squad dined on unlimited lamb (1-4)

38. Brian Greer, as 'Brendan'
In the *Guardian*, 2012

ACROSS
1 Citizen of UK, possibly born outside it (6)
5 He and I fail to produce part of engine (8)
9 Chap writing War and Peace, for example (8)
10 Mostly mature, but upset by a shocking experience (6)
11 Flaws in church's positions, by popular account (12)
13 Dreadfully evil (4)
14 Mistreat grandfather, say, concerning orchestral part (8)
17 Idiot breaking rule put in new post (8)
18 Be inclined to make record (4)
20 British flee in all directions, to town in part of Canada (3,9)
23 Bird turned over eggs etc. when disturbed (6)
24 Showing some Picasso on a screen, once (2,4,2)
25 Takes chair, as 'e's surrounded by lots of lions (8)
26 Title holder uses it (6)

DOWN
2 Call and go round (4)
3 A couple of hunters, perhaps, who cheat? (3-6)
4 Deny any wrong, for example (6)
5 Pleasant listening – such as 1, 7, 13, 18, 21 and 26, say? (5,2,4,4)
6 Legal officials like Leo and ten others (8)
7 Dictator, none the less, abandoned European currency (5)
8 Flexibility of wings, say, wrapped round seabirds (10)
12 Person with convictions? Yes and no (4-6)
15 Present knight after thriving king celebrated (4-5)
16 Having a specific position and special duties over a short time (8)
19 Stick unusually hard, as tacky stuff (6)
21 Players picked for defending champions (5)
22 Finish off *Guardian*, for example, in Irish house (4)

(continued from page 89)

"As for solving, these days I mostly do the *New York Times*. Monday through Thursday, they have themes, and I look for ideas I can pinch or adapt."

Here are a couple of Brian Greer's favourite clues:

1 In which three couples get together for sex (5)
2 The third letter after Q (10)

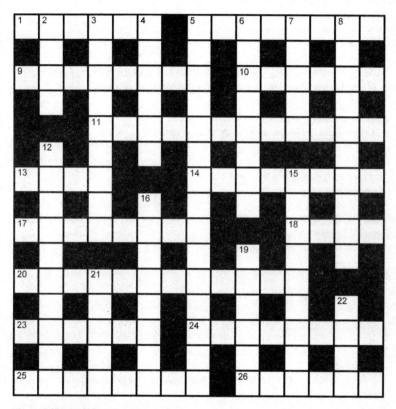

First published in the *Guardian* newspaper.

BERNICE GORDON

Ninety-nine years of age at the time of writing, Bernice has been penning crosswords for the *New York Times* since the very beginning in 1942, and can rightly claim to be a pioneer of creative crossword construction in the United States and beyond. Her 100th birthday, January 11, 2014, means she is just three weeks younger than the crossword!

Bernice explains how things were at the very start.

"Back in the '40s the editor was the wonderful Margaret Farrar. After writing for her for a number of years, I sent her a puzzle using ampersands instead of words – there were entries such as 'Carmen Mir&a', 'Sc&inavians', etc.

"Margaret was positively horrified! It had never been done before, and she felt it was not 'legal'. She asked if she could hold it for a while to reconsider.

'When she finally put it in the Sunday *NYT,* it caused havoc. She received hundreds of letters, which she forwarded to me. Some loved it, while others said it was cheating. After that, however, the rebus became part of crossword puzzling, and I am its mother.'

And Bernice is still producing quality work well into the twenty-first century.

"Crossword puzzles are the most important part of my life. My head is certainly still working!

"And I do a weekly puzzle for a group of solvers in the building where I live.

Here I am, old and grey, but full of piss and vinegar, and doing a new puzzle every day for my various editors.

"I am content and happy, and thank my lucky stars that I am still young at heart."

MATT GAFFNEY

Forty-year-old Matt, born in Washington DC, now living in the Shenandoah Valley of Virginia, describes himself as 92.5 per cent geek and 7.5 per cent total badass. A constructor for, among others, the *New York Times* and *Los Angeles Times,* Matt says that as more and more people are solving online, nowadays he focuses his attention more on crossword apps and his websites.

His first crossword was published when he was aged only 13 in the now defunct *Dell Champion Crossword Puzzles.*

"I was hooked right away" he enthuses, "and now it's unimaginable to me that I won't always be writing crosswords as long as I have a pulse." Matt describes his developing style over the years:

"The two major shifts in my style have happened because of technology. I used to write a lot of freestyle (aka 'themeless') puzzles but quit around 2000 because databases had gotten so large and high-quality that you had constructors I'd never heard of turning out these beautiful grids with the push of a button. So shift #1 is that I stopped writing freestyles; the corollary part of that is that I began writing meta-crosswords. The computers had taken the grid-filling part of crosswords away from me, so I showed them by emphasizing themes and clues, the two parts they can't touch. That's why my meta-puzzles are so popular, I think; it rehumanizes the art form, which also makes for better entertainment.

"People always ask: do you start with the grid or the clues? I say, neither. You start with a paying customer. But once that's taken care of, it's like building a house: put the big beams in first (that is, the long theme entries) and then fill the smaller ones in around it.

"And I must add, I get a lot of texts from people who are half way through a game of Scrabble!"

So how do you solve a meta-puzzle?

There are three basic steps:

Read the instructions
Each meta-puzzle comes with a set of unique instructions, such as 'This crossword's meta-answer is a city in Europe' or 'This crossword's meta-answer is a well-known TV show'. Make sure to read the instructions first so you know what you're looking for.

Solve the crossword
Solve it just as you would a regular crossword, but keep an eye out for anything unusual such as a clue that doesn't make sense, perhaps, or words with strange letter combinations like QDOBA or HAWAIIAN. These may (or may not!) have something to do with the meta.

Figure out the meta
It's a little tricky to give advice for this step since the meta-puzzle's trick can take many forms (and part of the fun is figuring out *what* you're supposed to be figuring out!), but after a few metas you'll catch on. Here's a tip: look at the title of the puzzle and the theme entries (theme entries are generally the longest entries in the grid). These are usually hints as to what's going on.

39. First-Quarter Action
By Matt Gaffney

'This meta answer is the answer to a hidden trivia question.'

Reprinted with kind permission of Matt Gaffney.

ACROSS

1 Pom or pug
4 Traditionally red transportation (not this one; go to 4-down)
9 Refuse
14 Roadside rescuers
15 Slowly destroy
16 "What is it, caller?"
17 It mentions the Isle of Wight (first quarter; then first quarter)
20 Prison system
21 First name in Oscar hosts

22 Switch settings
23 Like wallflowers
25 Piece of fruit that also just happens to be a common color
28 Part of the Dead Man's Hand (first quarter, then first quarter)
34 Ballyhoo
35 Said bad words
36 "Seriously!"
40 Enjoy your Kindle
42 Plunders
44 Drink named for part of the Florida Coast
45 Diet whose name means 'old'
47 Tan/gray hue
49 *The Simpsons* small business owner
50 NCAA Men's Division I Championship teams who've won their first two games, collectively (first quarter, then first quarter)
53 Golf gimmes
56 "You can stop telling me this now"
57 She said of her frequent inclusion in crosswords: "They just use my name as a filler"
58 Way
62 Scary snake
66 Duration of solitude, in a literary title (first quarter, then first quarter)
70 Uses a stopwatch
71 Man's name that's also a month
72 1004
73 Five-letter pronoun
74 Holiday feast
75 Angel dust

DOWN

1 Cooler version of 1-across
2 State quarter with this island's outline? It's Hawaii
3 Manxman, e.g.
4 Features a gym is very likely to have
5 One of a bodily pair
6 Former CIA head Porter _
7 Dim 1-across
8 "Who's up?"
9 Your of yore
10 Clipping caller
11 Crazy as _
12 Tossed
13 Basketball game
18 West Virginia-born Nobelist (in the fake Economics category, though)
19 Grand
24 Loud shout
26 _ single
27 Opens the bidding at
28 Virgil or Morgan at Tombstone
29 Brainstorm
30 Pitch point
31 Civil war historian Shelby _
32 Zagreb denizen
33 Words usually contracted
37 City with a University of Alaska satellite campus
38 First _ (orchestra chair)
39 Band with Dean and Gene
41 South Asian
43 Expectorate, less delicately
46 Have
48 Rudy Giuliani or David Dinkins
51 'Around the Horn' channel
52 High or low
53 'Chopper'
54 Musical redhead
55 Wordsworth words
59 Black and blue are two: Abbr.
60 'Good point'
61 Possessed
63 Not quite dry
64 Holder of much power in DC
65 Send regrets, say
67 Nervous chuckle
68 Put to work
69 Reno roller

SARAH HAYES
At the time of writing, Sarah is the only woman setting for *The Times*. She is Arachne in the *Guardian* and Anarche in the *Independent*.

Not only a fine setter, she is also the author of *A Study of English Nautical Loanwords in the Russian Language of the Eighteenth Century,* which according to Sarah contains the 'deathless definition' 'Upper futtock: any futtock other than the ground or lower futtock'. Her tome, she adds, has won 'Most Boring Book' at the Omsk Publishing Oscars.

At the time of writing, Sarah is the women's world-record holder for running a marathon dressed as a bottle.

When she set her first crossword, which appeared in the *Independent Saturday Magazine* in 1996, she was a keen amateur weaver (or "good at looming", as one friend put it), so that interest, together with the image of nervous and perhaps unsuspecting victims being ineluctably lured into the crossword setter's web, led her to choose 'Arachne' as her nom de guerre.

"When I started at the *Guardian* I stuck with Arachne as my moniker, but on joining the *Independent* in 2011 Arachne became Anarche (pronounced with three syllables) because as well as being a crossword setter I'm also proud founder of the Anarcho-Horizontalist Party. Anarcho-Horizontalism is a movement, or a lack of movement if you want to be picky, which aims to improve society by getting everyone to lie down a lot and do as little as possible, which is the answer to most problems, I find."

The Spiderwoman paints a vivid picture of her day: "As Spider Towers is the home of Anarcho-Horizontalism, a good part of my day is spent either in complete chaos, or lying down, or – most often – both."

And routine is not a familiar concept in the Arachne household.

"By noon, and still in my dressing gown, I've usually managed to remember what I'm supposed to be doing that day and, horror of horrors, whether there is a deadline looming. Crossword work isn't usually done to a timetable, but the word puzzle apps I write for a US software company involve contractual deadlines. Deadlines! No wonder these excrescences contain the word 'dead': it won't be booze or laziness that sends me to an early grave; it'll be a deadline. Hate 'em.

"At some point, after a minimum of three mugs of tea, Mr A will bring me breakfast in my office, which is the right hand end of the sofa, and work will commence, i.e. the computer gets switched on. Until about three years ago my setting was done with a black ink pen and a sheaf of good quality paper, but the Dear Leader (crossword editor) Hugh Stephenson tactfully pointed out that most other setters had long since gone over to the dark side and installed Crossword Compiler software on a new-fangled bit of kit called a computer. The hint was taken, with the result that I've subsequently spent a fortune on a series of laptops after variously spilling liquid on keyboards (gin and IT?), leaving the machine unsupervised in the presence of grandchildren, and the odd late night incidence of violence (is there anything more recalcitrant than a computer in a huff?).

"Mr A's office is at the other end of the sofa and, as the day progresses, he gradually disappears behind a wall of dictionaries, thesauruses and half-eaten sandwiches. I always stop for *Coronation Street*, and then more often than not I'll work through until the early hours."

C.G. RISHIKESH

In India the crossword community is relatively small, but expanding.

Having just turned 70, C.G. Rishikesh, aka Gridman, is senior crossword setter for the *Hindu*.

Here he responds at length to a question from crossword expert and ace blogger Shuchi Upadhyay, on www.crosswordsunclued.com: "What does it mean to be a crossword setter in India, and how do people respond when you tell them about your profession?"

"Well, first of all, I wouldn't say I am a professional crossword setter. For me, a professional crossword setter is one who gets all his earnings by setting crosswords. I would like to say I am a published crossword setter who gets paid for his work. What I get per puzzle is just a fraction of what a UK or US setter gets. I am not complaining, only putting things in the right perspective.

"Having said that, even in those countries, professional setters are likely to be far fewer than regular or hobbyist setters.

"Frankly speaking, I rarely tell anyone that I am a crossword setter. Honestly, it's often my wife who tells others that I am. She seems to be prouder than I am about the fact that I am a puzzler.

"As a matter of fact, for several years the publication where my crosswords appear used to carry the feature anonymously. I was quite comfortable with it. For me all the fun (along with the inevitable toil) was in the making of the crossword, not in the charm of seeing a by-line in print.

"But now the paper publishes crosswords with by-lines and every setter uses a pseudonym rather than an actual name.

"Whether crosswords have by-lines or not, I am sure regular solvers can identify a crossword setter by the cluing technique alone. The mere preponderance of a particular clue type could be a marker; or the repeated use of a component (such as 'support' or 'supporter' for BRA); or a sprinkling of smut in the clues; or perhaps the use of a theme with some clues asterisked.

"In India it's only a very small percentage of readers who solve crosswords in their newspaper. And an even smaller percentage of them would have the time or patience to complete the puzzle. For most it's an agreeable way of keeping themselves occupied for a few minutes before they dress up and go to college or work. To them, a setter – who is their opposite in this two-person game – is someone to be held in reverence. They will pardon even his occasional slips, knowing that the few Indian newspapers that carry original crosswords have no 'crossword editor' in the real sense of the term, and the onus is on the lonely setter.

40. The *Hindu*, 2012
by Gridman

ACROSS

6 No doubt about News Editor being dirt remover (7)

7 Make a speech to only half of the voters (5)

9 Against not one insect (3)

10 They are enlightened demons leaving multidimensional sections (10)

11 Decline to iron? (8)

13 Research paper of the half-sister (6)

15 Nobody but a religious woman is heard (4)

17 Edge towards 50 inside (5)

18 Be effusive about gloomy one getting head start (4)

19 Add up to a group of hands, we hear (6)

20 Deceit in West Indian business on ship (8)

23 Tuneful toy (7,3)

26 More apt to lose both ends? Feel sorry (3)

27 Something sticky in drug and lime concoction (5)

28 Crook Al breaking rowboat device (7)

DOWN

1 European with starry eye, properly presented recently (10)

2 New York tribe gets no idea out (6)

3 River rising in spectacular upper reaches (4)

4 Moving to remote sleeping unit (8)

5 Sound alarm about fighting by extreme ruffian (4)

6 Don't go on with Central leader's well-being (5)

8 Involves guts to extinguish right (7)

12 Send now without headers the message 'Provide funds' (5)

14 Ignore omen manifesting in part of ship (6,4)

16 Officer Commanding variously clued in to cover a passage (7)

17 I, a censor, revised the film script (8)

21 Scholar with great interest losing son for unknown comfort (6)

22 Trim ship parts from bottom upwards (5)

24 Article I encountered is facing the wrong way (4)

25 Almost bar allied group (4)

"In India, when one meets a setter, one is full of respect and awe. People think 'How can that small head carry so much that he knows?'. (Google and software are far from their minds.)

"In gatherings I have often had the experience of someone calling me by my real name and then introducing me to the accompanying person (wife or sister or even mother) as the pseudonymous setter. She tilts her head and warbles

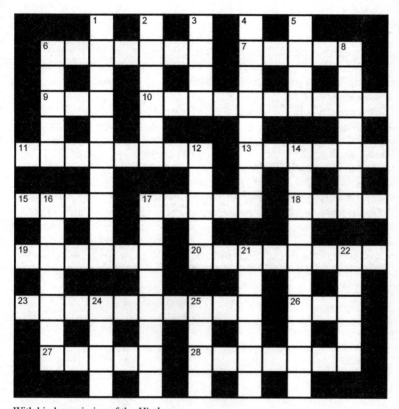

With kind permission of the *Hindu*.

out her approbation. One more admirer is notched up! This has been happening to me only recently, what with blogs and newspaper articles and the apparent spread of crossword lore.

"But in that moment of recognition I am not heading for cloud nine. Instead, my sense of responsibility increases and I am anxious that the next crossword that I set is free of error."

MERL REAGLE

According to puzzle constructor Merl Reagle, who constructs for many top newspapers across America, many of the writers behind the animation phenomenon that is *The Simpsons* are crossword fans. It stands to reason; the scriptwriters are brilliant wordsmiths themselves.

And Merl was soon to shoot to superstardom with his appearance on the cult show on November 16, 2008. He takes up the story on his website www.sundaycrosswords.com:

"A lot of the people who work on *The Simpsons* had seen *Wordplay* [a hugely entertaining movie based around the American Crossword Puzzle Tournaments] and liked it, and the show's main producer James L. Brooks suggested that Lisa should become hooked on crosswords and enter a crossword competition."

The episode's writer Tim Long sent Merl a script and it was read on a flight to Philadelphia. "I can't tell you how 'uptown' it felt not only to be reading a script on a plane, but a Simpsons script to boot, and one that was about crossword puzzles."

Asked to write a puzzle to accompany the show, Merl says, "I originally thought it would be a chance to hide a lot of character names through the puzzle – like 'Lisa' in PALISADE, 'Moe' in AMOEBA, etc."

"But this ended up as a secondary idea – something to spot, perhaps, after watching the episode. You can read out a diagonal message in the completed puzzle, and the first letters of the clues spell a message as well. A third idea is that the puzzle's theme of changing people's last names for humorous effect echoes what Lisa does when she learns that Homer bet against her in the crossword competition, changing her surname to 'Bouvier'!"

PAUL BRINGLOE
aka Neo, Tees

"I got into crosswords by smashing my face into a rugby post.

"So off to jolly old Odstock Hospital I went to get the mess fixed, and after the relevant surgical intervention – face in a Fernando Torres mask – I saw it on the rest room table: *Guardian* crossword puzzle set by Araucaria. So I picked it up, read a few clues, and was gobsmacked for the second time in as many weeks. This one stood out:

> Incredibly big nun caught student taking writing material without batting an eyelid (10)

"What? But crosswords are BORING: they don't have Pythonic silliness like that surely? And why the hell is it UNBLINKING? Well, who knows, but in the partially finished grid, that answer was all that would fit. And so I was hooked.

"Years later, I met a very silly man at *The Times* Crossword Championships by the name of John Halpern. So I said to him, 'hey John, how about a chat about some of my puzzles that I think are brilliant?' And he hit me with a fire extinguisher. Nevertheless he was kind enough to sit with me, at length, and on more than one occasion, to help improve my absolutely appalling efforts.

"Why did he do that? Well, suffice it to say that I did – eventually – release his mother and sister from their captivity in my shed, but only after he had seen and changed ALL my clues. I am grateful to him.

"What am I? An advertising copywriter for Saatchis, O&M, various others: a drummer in a prog band called The Far Meadow, and wife and mother of six. I set for The *FT*, the *Indy*, and *The Times*.

"Style? I think I'm fair, but others say I'm ginger. Actually I really hate bad cryptic grammar, so imagine the artistic pain I'm almost constantly in.

"I hate grids that isolate the four corners, and Portsmouth Football Club, with a vengeance."

ROGER SQUIRES

Living in the beautiful and historic English town of Ironbridge, Shropshire, Roger Squires is extraordinarily prolific, and has been dubbed the 'Mozart of Crosswords'.

A former member of the Magic Circle, he appeared on many Rolf Harris shows and on the children's show *Crackerjack*, and his versatility stretched to a three-month spell as an actor in the long-gone cardboard-walled, motel-based British soap opera *Crossroads*, playing Amy Turtle's nephew.

It surely is no coincidence that Roger has entered the *Guinness Book of World Records* on a number of occasions as the world's most prolific crossword compiler. Perhaps, just perhaps, March 9, 1961 proved a defining moment, providing the impetus to open the door to the rich and varied life he has evidently lived, and the drive to be so prolific.

With thanks to Shuchi Upadhyay and her interview at www.crosswordsunclued.com, Roger takes up his remarkable story:

"On March 9, 1961 I was acting as fighter-controller in an AEW Gannet aircraft about to land on *HMS Hermes* at sea off Ceylon – now Sri Lanka. The aircraft stalled at 300 feet [90 m] and the right wing fell and broke off as we hit the sea, turning us upside-down. As we sank we could hear the ship's propellers very near to us. I pulled the lever that should blow off the small door to the controllers' compartment – the size of the two front seats of a small car – but no movement resulted. I took off my parachute and, as the water covered my face, hung from the roof kicking at the door. As the incoming sea-water equalized the sea pressure outside, the door floated away. I took a last breath from the small pocket left above me and dived out. Once free of the aircraft I inflated my Mae West and rapidly moved upwards in darkness. I recall a huge feeling of delight as the light became brighter and brighter and I popped up on the surface at such a speed that only my feet didn't leave the water. My eyes suddenly blurred as aviation fuel covered my eyes but on wiping them clear I could see the rescue helicopter hovering above me. Two minutes later I was back on board. Sadly the pilot had been killed.

"It was established by later investigation that I escaped from more than 60 feet [18 m] below the surface. At no time during the crash did I feel frightened or worried; I just followed the actions learned in repeated training. For days afterwards, every time I leant forward water gushed out from my sinuses, which was somewhat embarrassing. It was only later that I realized how lucky I was. Before the accident I was a bit of a worrier, but since then I have taken life far more light-heartedly."

Roger is jolly and approachable, as are his puzzles, deemed by many to be excellent for the beginner. He is the master of the cryptic definition and never over-complicates his clues. He is often published at the start of the week when it is considered solvers don't need their brains taxed too much. This is much like in the US, where puzzles are often referred to as being of 'Friday difficulty' or at 'Tuesday level'.

Here Roger paints a picture of his day:

"When I started setting, I used to sit in the living room, drawing out the grids and filling in solutions with pencil and rubber. When my first wife came, with a young son, I found it difficult to work with my concentration being disturbed and used the spare bedroom as an office. When she left I had to spend a lot of time looking after the two boys, washing, cooking, etc and finally converted an outbuilding into a cottage where, in lieu of rent, a housekeeper could help out.

"I then made a room at the end of the garage into an office and, with the need to earn money from low-fee syndicated puzzles, I felt I needed a structured day. I took the children to school after breakfast, then went into the office from about 9 a.m. and worked until 1 p.m. Then it was lunch and rest before they returned from school, and back to work from 4.30 to 6.30 p.m.'

Now in his eighties, Roger is still working these basic hours "… and Anna [his wife] often comments how structured I am!

"I do like to complete a crossword before leaving the office, or I find it affects my sleep if I am trying to think of unfinished clues. I start with the long words in a grid and never insert another word to be clued until I have written the existing ones. This often means that if I cannot find a clue that works in a particular puzzle I write the unused clues down on a list to be used for future crosswords.

"My office is small, which means everything is within reach. It's crammed with reference books, and my index system in which I put every clue I use, with date and outlet. When a new clue is required, and I am stuck, a glance through the clues for a word often sparks off a new idea or combination."

Roger's record-breaking antics extend to his *Guinness Book of World Records* entry for the longest word in a puzzle. Llanfairpwllgwyngyllgogerychwrndrobwllllantysiliogogogoch, a Welsh village, is known to the locals as LLANFAIR PG.

The crossword on which a Hove woman wrote her last wishes (more on which we shall discover later in this book) was one of Roger's. On that occasion, Roger claims to have been a bit disappointed that Aunty Nettie, aged 99, had only half finished the straight crossword, and had not attempted Roger's more challenging cryptic effort.

"I suppose her mind was on other things," he says.

41. Roger Squires
The Birmingham Post, July 1970

ACROSS

1 Eve, for example, had only one conviction (5,8)
10 Such an entrance confuses singers (7)
11 Quite different people have it in common (7)
12 A bird watcher never conceals it (4)
13 A full round or a small portion? (5)
14 Don't go to give support (4)
17 It's mean to keep a girl in such a long time (7)
18 Poem about our dean (7)
19 Not an inside job, apparently (7)
22 It's obvious I'd entered a contest (7)
24 Inclination to drive home quietly (4)
25 Separate verse form (5)
26 Still not excited (4)
29 After wine, I join the company in the porch (7)
30 He helps a superior, we hear? (7)
31 Drink to lay one down? (8,5)

DOWN

2 Genuine form of an actress (7)
3 Staunch support (4)
4 Comment on what you see? (7)
5 Does he only imagine himself interested in birds? (7)
6 Put down some money (4)
7 How a pet lies when it is penned (7)
8 It helps one realize projected amusement (13)
9 Dangerous antagonists waiting at the beauty parlour? (4,9)
15 Bird in top gear, apparently? (5)
16 A forger's block (5)
20 Thanks to a French sailor, a monkey appears (7)
21 How to sing a piece written in quavers? (7)
22 A gentle arrangement exhibiting good taste (7)
23 Commodity excessively used (7)
27 An element of jazz in classical music (4)
28 Country in which hope runs high (4)

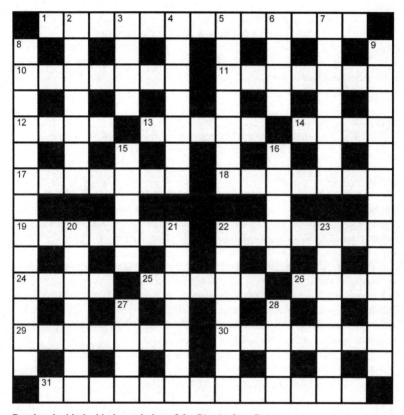

Reprinted with the kind permission of the *Birmingham Post*.

JOHN YOUNG

Audrey and John Young are mother and son setters for the *Guardian*, as Audreus and Shed, respectively. Whenever an Audreus puzzle appears, *Guardian* aficionados can expect to be solving a Shed on the following day. John is also published under the name Dogberry in the *Financial Times*.

My first meeting with Cambridge research associate John Young was an eye-opener. It had not even occurred to me that crossword setters would drink beer. That hazy afternoon I (vaguely) remember asking Shed about his pseudonym. I had imagined him with a wife fed-up with his crossword obsession, banishing him to the bottom of his garden to pen his masterpieces upon a soiled bench, his companions the lawn-mower and a rusty trowel or two. It seems I was wrong.

He looks like a shed.

John takes up the story:

"'Shed' is a nickname conferred on me by a friend at university who was a rather gifted cartoonist and produced a caricature of me as a garden shed. The name had fallen out of use by 1984, when my first puzzle was published and I rather missed it, so I decided to resurrect it. 'Dogberry' wasn't actually my idea, it was suggested by the *Financial Times* crossword editor. Dogberry is the incoherent police officer in Shakespeare's *Much Ado About Nothing*, of whom another character complains 'This learned constable is too cunning to be understood'. I've since discovered that at least two other compilers had used the pseudonym before I did.

"I fill in grids at home and write clues, for the most part, in the pub. But ideas for clues can come at any time, even in your sleep."

I do remember during our first encounter John telling me that he had been asked to remove the following (quite brilliant) clue from one of his submitted *Guardian* puzzles, as at the time he wrote it, the mid 1980s, the subject matter might be seen as inciting violence! Well, you'd think this wasn't possible, but as we shall read later crosswords can certainly prove fatal. Here's the clue:

1 Ludicrous toll causing breach of the peace (4,3)

And here's another of Shed's (arguably also politically incorrect) favourite clues:

2 He hasn't been all there since the operation! (7)

THE TOUGH GUYS

Dean Mayer and John Henderson are British setters at the scary end of the solving spectrum:

DEAN MAYER

A number of setters across the world have a reputation for being a little tougher than the average setter. One such is Dean Mayer, a setter for *The Times*, also known as Anax in the *Independent*.

Dean takes his pseudonym from a reversal of his daughter's name Xana. He is also Loroso in the *Financial Times* and Elkamere in the *Daily Telegraph*.

In his spare time he is the bassist for the top-notch funk and disco band Le Funk (which played at my wedding).

Back in the early 1960s Dean's pregnant mother was prescribed the morning sickness drug thalidomide, later found to be the cause of birth defects. Dean was born with one hand.

"Luckily, my mum heard about its effects almost immediately, so she stopped. Unlike others who really suffered, I escaped with just an absence of fingers on my left hand and a brain wired to play with crosswords at some future point in my life.

"It makes playing the bass tricky at times because I only have a thumb available to hit the strings – and there is the financial side-effect in that I'm forced to play a left-handed bass, and they're more expensive. I'd started as the (mid-teens) singer in my very first band, and when it became apparent that I couldn't sing I had the choice either to play something or sod off. The guys suggested I play bass, and that was it. I thought, 'Play a guitar? With only half a set of fingers? This'll be a laugh.'"

Dean's always up for a challenge – as are his solvers.

Here he describes his style:

"The only way I can describe it is 'me'. There isn't an effort to *be* anything in particular, and that's probably a healthy approach.

"The cryptic setter has a generous but finite set of tools to work with. To apply something based on my own personality imposes another restriction. For me, I just start playing around with definitions and wordplay components and see what can be strung together coherently. If there is a shade of personal colour, that only comes about because certain definitions or wordplay indicators will be more appealing to me than others, but that's due to an inbuilt set of subconscious rules and I'm not really aware of them. That said, in terms of a finished product I place a convincing surface reading (the story told by the clue) above everything else, which I suppose you could call a 'style'."

Dean is being modest. He is a master at running the definition and the cryptic part of clues together so seamlessly that it's often impossible to see the join.

(continued on page 110)

42. Anax
The Independent, 2012

ACROSS

1/3 Swim, as do (and are) eight clues (4,10)

10 In France most of you will have expensive ticket (7)

11 The wagon is not carrying metal (7)

12 What we can learn from fossils or ruins that lay scattered? (7,7)

13 Church blocks intelligence more or less (5)

14 Clergywoman interferes with small group from the east (9)

17 A politician in training to have clique's indulgence (9)

19 Extra turned into an extra (3-2)

21 Cook the gerbil with a fresh vegetable (5,9)

25 National Airlines to drop new bombs (7)

26 Much about turning behind to medium size here? (3,4)

27 Ship loaded with ancient Byzantine spades (10)

28 Soldier on when losing mother? (4)

DOWN

1 See, French wine's good – see raised trophy (6,3)

2 Caught one trying to bag rabbit (7)

4 Flynn, actor making comeback (5)

5 Maturity affects me, suppressing fashionable illusion? (9)

6 Part of picture, name regularly seen within it (5)

7 Local do – goes topless to provide stimulation (7)

8 Massage given to auditor (4)

9 Form of identification accepted by bank (8)

14 It could be inoperative if all traces of earth are removed (9)

15 Detailed evidence in horrifying case (8)

16 Protective cover confirmed without UN control (3,6)

18 Reason for alarm, perhaps, over one heading for Africa? (7)

20 Designer, American, starts to make a scene (7)

22 Beef sandwich, and each filling (5)

23 It ultimately kills aristos (5)

24 Racing driver gets one for nothing (4)

(continued from page 109)

Asked to come up with a couple of clues of which he is proud, Dean cites: 'Mister Bob Hope (7)'. "The answer is SPRAYER – something that creates a mist, or a 'mister'. Then it's s (bob as in shilling) and PRAYER ('hope' as in 'You haven't got a hope'). It isn't actually a spectacular clue, but it stands out for me because it was written for a word that forced itself into the grid – anything else would have been too obscure – and I'd expected to struggle with it. Yet the

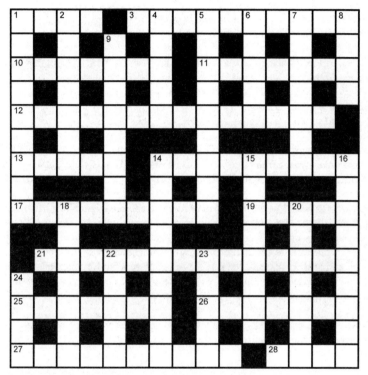

Reprinted with kind permission of the *Independent* newspaper.

components simply leapt out with almost no thought, an absolute gift. Some clues can take an hour or so to hone into something that ticks a few quality boxes; this took no more than 30 seconds and that alone makes it perfect in my book."

The other he mentions is:

'Ace used in variety of snap – the game (8)', or PHEASANT.

Which unravels as: 'A' for Ace inside an anagram of 'SNAP THE'.

"Here, the definition is disguised because both 'ace' and 'snap' persuade the solver to think of a card game."

JOHN HENDERSON

When asked why people describe his crosswords as tough, John (aka Enigmatist, Nimrod, Elgar and Io) answers in a matter-of-fact manner, "Probably because they are."

"I honestly don't set out to make them tough. I tap into an eclectic range of general knowledge, but that's how I myself learned to do crosswords."

And John started young. I mean, really young, first getting published as Enigmatist in the *Guardian* at the age of 15.

"My mum and dad were, of course, very proud, but I think schoolmates were quite suspicious of someone who compiled crosswords for the school mag at the age of nine."

These days John's preferred place of work is any one of a number of pubs around the north of London. "There's a thriving community at our weekly solvers and setters get-togethers. People like doing cerebral things over a pint," he adds.

John Henderson is one quarter of the 'setter' for the *Guardian* called Biggles. Around once a year for the last five years or so, John Henderson, John Graham (Araucaria), John Young (Shed) and myself, John Halpern, combine to write a quarter of a puzzle each.

But why Biggles? Well, the stories of flying ace Cecil Wigglesworth, aka Biggles, written from 1932 onwards and loved by schoolboys during my youth, were penned by one W.E. Johns. Johns was a fascinating man in his own right, who once managed to crash three planes on consecutive days. Furthermore, it is an administrative headache for 'we Johns' to get paid for this more-or-less annual collaboration. Instead, we are taken for a free meal at a pub in the Bedfordshire town of ... (wait for it!) Biggleswade.

Overleaf is one of John Henderson's marvellous head-scratchers, appearing under the pseudonym Nimrod (the most famous of Elgar's *Enigma Variations*).

Here are some all-time favourite clues, as chosen by John Henderson:

A delightful 'say what you see', from Araucaria:

1   Ofofofofofofofofof (10)

A Delhi belly laugh from Enigmatist:

2   Where to find Ali G after very hot curry? (8)

Not a lot you can say about this, also from Enigmatist:

3   I say nothing (3)

An e-fission-t clue from Peter Chamberlain for the *Daily Telegraph:*

4   Nuclear rabbit? (4-7)

One from an eye-twinklingly lovely friend, Albie Fiore, who left us far too soon:

5   No can do (6,5)

Some Church of England smut from Araucaria:

6   Impossible to express in a four-letter word? (9)

Les May, Azed prizewinning clue, and favourite clue of many crossword setters.

7   Bust down reason? (9)

A stunningly inventive swerve from Enigmatist:

8   The real reason for the merger meeting between Volkswagen and Daimler? (6,6)

The late and brilliant *Guardian* setter Bunthorne, aka Bob Smithies, said a most treasured possession was a fan letter from Araucaria, who loved this next clue of his, also a favourite of John Henderson:

9   Amundsen's forwarding address (4)

43. Nimrod
The Independent, December 31, 2009

ACROSS
1 Retired, a head wants to get back to work... (7)
5 ... here, with year of high rank? (6)
10 Nonsense written into Tablet 4 (7)
11 This time runner makes it in close (3,4)
12 What one needs to know to become an England bowler? (6)
13 Excellent conductor of liquid or steam (7)
15 Woman with figure repeatedly noted leader of 6 (7)
20 No-no? Could be positive as well as negative (3-4)
25 Plant flower in grass (7)
26 Wait on some news now date's on (6)
28 See 2 Down
29 In viva, a little circuitous (7)
30 Queen making such profit?... (6)
31 ... in respect of single *Crush* (7)

DOWN
1 Cut of beef sparking bar riots (3,5)
2/28/3 19's explanation for missing acrosses: the river current floods paper hanging interminably (3,5,4,3,1-7)

4 I'm occupying Mother Earth (4)
6 Posse arresting setter in possession of grass (6)
7 Free and easy, he leaves the elves dancing (6)
8 Fret about a climbing plant (6)
9 End of tube to put right up, dispensing fluid finally (5)
14 Swear after-effects could be two much either way (3)
16 'Quite a few' topped 'some' (3)
17 Beds where I am – daughter's not likely to change (8)
18 Writer banged up in compound after beginning to serve several months? (8)
19 Boy band having problems accommodating Lemonheads' lead singer (3,5)
21 The second coffee recipe (6)
22 Result of 14 having so-called 'treatment' (6)
23 Star student (tenor) negotiating a melody (6)
24 No longer bright classes struggling to fuel interest for a short time (5)
27 Timeless plaything repeatedly changing direction (2-2)

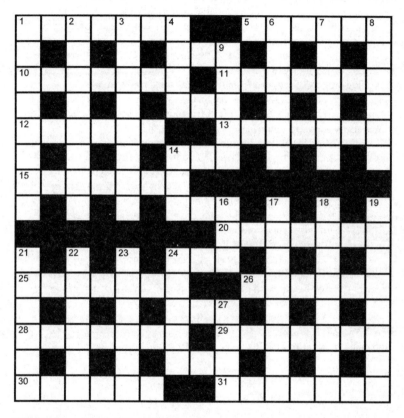

With kind permission of the *Independent* newspaper.

THE TOUGHEST OF THE TOUGH

If you thought the last two puzzles were 'a challenge' meet:

The *Listener* crossword.

The dedicated *Listener* solver, often after weeks of perseverance (!), will seek to slowly unravel a devious preamble, and unlock the secrets of this labyrinthine work of genius. The *Listener* certainly is the daddy of them all, and the mother of all crosswords.

The Times and *Listener* setter and software engineer Roger Phillips explains the writing process:

"As for the process of setting a *Listener* puzzle, there really isn't one.

"The variety of themes should dictate that each puzzle's construction has to be approached in a relevant way. Any list of techniques must be incomplete, as the ideal is always to find a brand new idea that breaks the mould.

"For many of us, the ability to write software is an advantage, as it can enable tasks such as searching large word lists to find those that fit a certain theme, or working out grid manipulations that would take too long to find by hand.

"But many good themes don't require any of that, having grids that can be created by hand, albeit usually with a lot of patience. I think the programming mindset also lends itself well to the kinds of shenanigans that one expects in grids, but one of the beauties of the *Listener* is that setters come from all sorts of backgrounds and have different approaches."

One of Roger Phillips' *Listener*-style puzzles is on pages 118–119, written for the 2003 convention of the *National Puzzlers' League* in Indianapolis, Indiana. Designed for Americans, with US spellings, Roger used *Merriam-Webster's 10th Collegiate Dictionary* as his primary reference.

For reasons that will become obvious, Roger's usual pseudonym of Kea became 'Moa' for this puzzle.

Incidentally, what Brits call a 'pseudonym', Americans call a 'nom'.

XIMENEAN VS ARAUCARIAN

According to crossword.org.uk, otherwise known as the Crossword Centre, "Ximenes, Derrick Somerset Macnutt [whom we met earlier] set new standards in fairness and humour, and is considered, rightly, to be the father of the modern crossword puzzle."

Well, maybe. But it is the word 'rightly' with which I would take issue. 'Rightly' suggests those who disagree are wrong. But Ximenes certainly did lay down rules in his *Ximenes on the Art of the Crossword,* to which many top cryptic crossword setters adhere to this day.

However, it was Araucaria who advised this author never to read Ximenes' book.

I guess it's human nature to want to take sides, to sit comfortably in one camp among like-minded thinkers, speaking of our 'correct' way. We have an innate desire to be right about our views. But these are just our opinions, and no more important than that. Why is it that Araucaria is so often vilified by his peers, and yet almost universally lauded by crossword solvers? Having said all this, there is a lot to learn from Ximeneans.

In fact, the great Ximenean Mike Laws, late editor of *The Times* crossword and a first-rate crossword setter in his own right as Fawley in the *Guardian*, used to describe 'cryptic algebra' as his device for crossword setting.

Clues might be written in the forms: '$X + Y = Z$' as a charade, or '$Z = X/Y$' as a container type clue, for example, where Z is the definition and X and Y are the constituent parts of the wordplay.

Anyhow, nowadays things are different. I am married, and supposedly mature. My roving eye days are over – and now I am even considering buying my first pair of corduroy trousers. Is middle age here? Am I joining the establishment? Am I becoming … a Ximenean?

DON MANLEY

… discusses why he would firmly place himself in the Ximenean camp: "I choose to follow the fairness code expounded by Afrit, as developed by Ximenes and Azed, in respect of what can be considered fair and grammatically accurate. Others take a looser view of what can be judged acceptable. For the vast majority of clues there is no great problem, but there will always be areas of cluemanship on which crossworders differ. What I slightly resent is the accusation in some quarters that 'Ximeneans' are a humourless load of stuffy old classicists, devoid of fun, who haven't recognized that crossword clues have 'moved on' or 'evolved' – that is nonsense.

"Ultimately, it is the crossword editors who are the gate-keepers for what they regard as fair. While not all of them accept my strictures on fairness, they all (I am glad to say) respect the integrity of my own clue-writing."

(continued on page 122)

44. 'Kicking a Habit'
By Moa

ACROSS

5 Navy staff surrounds mostly sluggish, backward country (10, 2 words)

11 Port grows pallid in South Africa (7)

12 Multinational company is sort of light, holding nothing, right? (8)

13 Shift stain occurring annually (7)

14 Cross-town subway starting by four of farms using minimum labor (9)

15 Abdominal folds, curious to man (6)

16 Man's organ and small piano finally humor 'contrary' girl (8)

17 Possibly bumps up solution of starch with a bit of titration (8)

20 Alcoholic shaking about downpour alights from a coach (8)

23 Old pub landlord giving Alabama doctor a month (9)

29 Pair of cups of alloy, half iron (9)

30 Distraught, Sammy is hiding alkalinity count in lung condition (9)

31 Having sugar put in train driving past switch (9)

32 Fishy cooking in chips? Not half! (7)

33 Informant has run in with author printing slips (6)

34 Run through lap in shifting of parts in proximity to rump (8)

35 Auxiliary taking in round-trip in a watchful way (7)

36 Danish, say, adopting a low social class (9)

DOWN

1 Not part of standard Christian church, nor saint, anyhow (9)

2 Swam frantically, supporting normal navy anchor, possibly (7)

3 Happily, touchdown did pass out (7)

4 Chap who abruptly grasps awfully scant hour (8)

6 Spitwad shot up to your midriff (9, hyph.)

7 Forward-facing colonist is crying loudly, having lost adult (8)

8 Back of local pub hosts a thousand football forwards (7)

9 Not all of colonials acclaim Gallic location (6)

10 Surround Latin man in taboo, almost (7)

18 Stays dry, surprisingly, for past occasions (10)

19 Obstructs Janis, say, typical of an author (8)

21 Old habitations in Italy, thanks to British spoil around railroad (9)

22 Folks giving solution bring up strontium attaching to radical with sulfur and sodium (9)

24 Unusually primal capital of Honduras (7)

25 With T-shirt for tip of alp, Swiss ski town was maturing (8)

26 Still crazy about Morrison's last parts for Doors (7)

27 Syllogism's origin in contrary of that proposition put forward without proof (6)

28 Asian starling circling cloudy classical city (7)

You must modify any solution word going into this diagram by totally purging it of a drug. Cryptic indications match grid forms, not full words. A pair of diagonal words (10, 8) will show up finally, honouring your tribulations.

Reprinted with kind permission of Roger Phillips.

45. Don Manley, as Quixote
The Independent 1989

ACROSS

1 Valuables from when biblical community settled in wood? (9)

6 A cheese produced to roll around? (4)

10 Trouble-maker's past with leader of gang run in (5)

11 Study in group, right inside always and deskbound? (9)

12 Criticize zero thickness in suit of armour (7)

13 Sweetmeat, arabic, conveyed by ship of the desert (7)

14 Old hostilities that would presumably cause more than a marital itch? (5,5,3)

17 Behold 'chapel racer around'? (5,8)

21 Travel around accompanied by Napoleon's marshal in combat on horseback (7)

22 Dad, having terrible acne, needs a remedy (7)

24 Detects rickety transport on the river (9)

25 Drawing imitating Raphael in part (5)

26 Thanks volunteers in final salutation (4)

27 Oriental author grabs attention? The reverse (9)

DOWN

1 One allowing no words to escape from mouth, holy saint (8)

2 The Spanish drink making an appearance in Scottish town (5)

3 Moving quickly from place to place in trail about commercial area (14)

4 Model again needs break, see, having got upset (7)

5 Into which passenger goes for a drink (7)

7 Music for a solemn occasion when not even the daffodils come out? (4-5)

8 One's airborne briefly, but *could* plummet? (6)

9 He funded libraries, providing possibility of new reading with care (6,8)

15 Titbit that has little volume and an opening the content of which is superior? (3-2-4)

16 Gill maybe gets a rest (8)

18 Articles for baby not ready on time, yet to be collected (7)

19 Makes a second attempt to please the cameraman maybe and is still (7)

20 Thoroughfare in West Country town (6)

23 Take tea in a series of hotels, perhaps (5)

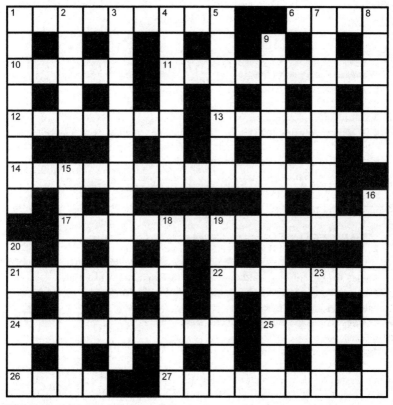

With kind permission of the *Independent*.

(continued from page 117)

And I'm sure Don is not wrong. Don's clues can all be parsed clearly and effectively, which on occasion is probably not so true of my own, where my thinking starts from 'what's fun', after which I make a considered judgment on the clue's fairness, and ask a friend's opinion, if needs be. If the friend laughs, it goes in; if they harrumph, it's out. But these instances are few, perhaps once per crossword? The rest I'd consider follow clear rules.

Don also lists what he considers to be a 'good' and a 'poor' clue:

What makes a good clue
1 Soundness of construction
2 Good surface meaning, including possible distraction from construction
3 Well-disguised definition
4 Disguised construction (not obvious what type of clue / seamless join between definition and rest of clue / shift in part of speech of a word in clue)
5 Novel element that isn't very hackneyed
6 Often short and pithy
7 Sometimes downright funny but more often tickling the intellect
8 Working out the components and the definition in a to-and-fro process

What makes a poor clue
1 No real sense other than as a crossword clue
2 Sloppy construction with bad grammar/unsound devices such as 'indeed' suggesting the solver should find something inside the word deed.
3 You get the answer (maybe from the definition) long before you remotely understand how the clue works
4 Going over the edge in crudeness/ bad taste

There is an example of Don's work on page 120.

On the other hand, here's a clue of mine: Entury? (4,4,2,3). The answer is: LONG TIME NO SEE. I hope it works – what do you think? Perhaps it's not Ximenean – there's not even a definition (!) – and I struggle to explain why I think it does work, so for those who need to validate each clue, you may be disappointed.

But, what is the secret of great crossword comedy? (1,6,1,4). I HAVEN'T A CLUE.

A few years back I remember solving this, from Araucaria:

Pretender misspelt with 4 U's? (5-2)

I had W-U-D-E, so it just *had* to be 'would-be', a pretender. But why 'misspelt with 4 u's?'. Well, 'misspelt' sounded rather like an anagram indicator…. but still, it was a full half hour later before I worked out that the letters to be jumbled were the 4 u's, or… DOUBLE W.

Not Ximenean. Not Ximenean at all.

Here are some words from John Graham, aka Araucaria, on what he calls:

THE XIMENEAN STRAITJACKET

"I cut my crossword teeth on Ximenes, 70 or so years ago, and remain full of admiration for his puzzles. Their erudition, wit, fairness, and originality set me a model which I have tried to follow ever since. Because he deliberately used as many obscure words as possible, the solver needed a clear set of logical rules for cluing, which his devotees gladly accepted when solving his puzzles. But to apply his rules to all cryptic crosswords is (in my view) unnecessary and unworkable.

"For most of us, most of the time, a few rare words may be OK but the fun lies in devising tricky clues to everyday words and phrases; and, if those clues are impressionistic rather than scientifically exact, no one but the pedant cares, so long as when the solution dawns it is manifestly right.

"And logic, in language, is inevitably subjective; it's 'each to his own'. Ximenes admits as much; in the chapter on 'cluemanship' in *Ximenes on the Art of the Crossword,* he tells us of his own disagreements with his forerunner Afrit's rules.

"A brief example: 'I am in the plot, that's clear' for PLA(I)N.

"For Ximenes, the letter 'I' and the person 'I' are not the same, so it should be 'I is' (so put 'I must be ... which is OK for both). For me, in the crossword world they are the same, so 'I am' is fine. Consider the 'head' clues which Ximeneans hate: 'Hammerhead' for H – OK because it means 'head of a hammer', but not 'Dunderhead' for D because it doesn't mean 'head of a dunder'? What about 'Gateshead'? You are entitled to make your own rules, but they can't apply across the board.

"All the same, I would side with the Ximeneans on some points where impressionism has gone too far: how can 'regularly' possibly indicate that you have to take every other letter of a word? If the answer is that it's an accepted crossword convention, I protest that it isn't fair to devise conventions that have no logic in them at all. They ought always to be such that a competently reasoning person who had no inside knowledge could eventually solve a puzzle. But, by the same token, it should not require adherence to an arbitrary set of rules."

In the same way we remember where we were at the moment of great and infamous moments in history, I remember exactly where I was on April 27, 1994. I was sitting in the car park of Christ's Church College, Canterbury – solving the crossword on the next page. I remember it clearly as a most powerful, exciting and moving experience, capturing perfectly the occasion of a nation's first democratic elections.

46. Araucaria
The Guardian, April 27, 1994

"A tribute on Election Day to the fighters for democracy, especially martyrs such as 6, 16 and 3."

ACROSS

1 The South country's a fair country, initially and potentially (6)

4 Ready now to be joined together around the start of a historic journey (7)

9 Going round a hill he's got on a coat of mail (9)

10 Alan the country lover goes to the back for approval (5)

11 Cask is in the 1 across (5)

12 Puce flesh, transformed, is expressive (9)

13 Big one at the theatre, short one at home (7)

15 Sort of theatre featuring an old maid around the South (6)

17 Mischievous attempt to silence Zulu warriors? (6)

19 Bled, laboured, wept, and ... (applied to labour) (7)

22 Natal is up for change, their projects were 15 (9)

24 Legally prevent some injuries to property (5)

26 Velocity and space cause engine noise (5)

27 Rely strangely on Italian money to be fit for the armed struggle? (9)

28 Data from transmitter for ultimate defence, remove (a) and insert (b) (4,3)

29 Biblical hero called Helen and Slovo (6)

DOWN

1 In a movie, having heat and not light? (7)

2 The bird, not the island (5)

3 In breaking of chain, the hour is here for him (5,4)

4 See 8

5 Subject at work in convulsive movement (5)

6 Bible book, opening chapter: compassion a priority (4,5)

7 Start of democracy – viewpoint put before enticingly (6)

8/4 Ex-prisoner takes hold; he cut short the wait (6,7)

14 Cyril's got a plan for some homelands in the country (9)

16 Proponent of consciousness, providing blacks evoke it (5,4)

18 Earphones for the leading group? (4-3)

19 Walter turned up in Zulus' island (6)

20 Artistic pair, as from Wilton, need 500-yard pitch (7)

21/23 Exile to be remembered, green at first, in the circle where things are forgotten (6,5)

25 The pain of birth or death, or the revolution (5)

ARAUCARIA

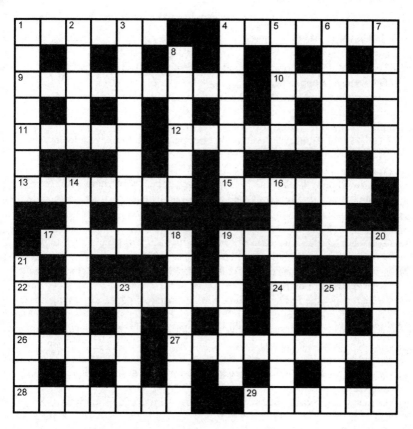

First published in the *Guardian* newspaper.

CHAPTER 8
THE SETTER'S MIND

A DAY IN A LIFE

Does this happen to you?

You're sitting in a restaurant, studying the menu.

The waitress approaches.

Her nametag tells you she is 'Melissa'.

You are immediately distracted. What you're saying, and what you're thinking are poles apart.

'Anagram of "aimless"', you think: 'Her parents should have known better.'

"What would you like today?" You study the menu:

You read: 'Pizza'.

You think: there is pizza in the horse, LiPIZZAner, a white horse. But is there horse in the pizza? There may well be – this is Britain.

You read: 'Four seasons'.

You think: double the salt and pepper?

You read: 'Pasta' – anagram of 'tapas', which is interesting as the staple dish of Italy anagrammatizes to that of Spain.

Mixed green salad – well, if I mix it I might get 'grease land'. Let's hope not.

To drink: Chardonnay.

Can you spot the rude word hidden in it? I once asked the same question of the charming former editor of *The Times* newspaper, James Harding, over a swanky – I shan't point that particular hidden word out – luncheon. James had been deep in conversation with another colleague, discussing the strategic deployment of British troops in the Helmand province of Afghanistan – I'd thought he needed some light relief. It was, in retrospect, a misjudgement.

Desserts – of course, 'stressed' backwards. All this makes me want to scream.

So ice cream for my order.

Or better still, I could order a dish that is an anagram of my drink ....

Before I digest, let me digress:

And so it was the moment I first set eyes on the lovely woman who was eventually to become my wife.

She introduced herself:

"I'm Taline."

Well, how would you have responded? "How exotic – I wonder where the name comes from?"

Probably. But those quite logical and natural thoughts are for normal people – whereas I write crosswords.

My thought? 'Anagram of "Entail"'.

This was not a thought to speak aloud. That would have been the end, surely.

Instead, I went for the more predictable, and safer, option of: "Beautiful name, and unusual. Where does the name come from?"

"Armenia," she responded.

"The word MEN inside the word ARIA", I thought. "Structurally very good for creating a cryptic clue."

But that's not how I replied.

"Oh, very interesting. Tell me more about Armenia ..."

... and so it continued.

On our first date we had briefly discussed what I do for a living, but I certainly didn't want to frighten her off. I left the killer observation for our first proper date.

We are in a Vietnamese restaurant. Vietnamese, as hidden in SOVIET NAME SErgey, the relevance of which eludes me, but I spot it anyway. There are king prawns on the menu. I seize my chance to impress her. I order them – and spring water for my drink.

I am nervous. What will she think? I really like this girl. She has gorgeous deep brown eyes, flowing black locks, a stunning and mischievous smile, and she's so stylish and unpretentious – a delight! But in order for 'us' to work, she has to 'get' me.

Our meals arrive, and we prepare to eat. I take a deep breath, and ...

"I was just wondering if you were aware – erm, probably not, but hey, I'm going to tell you anyway ..."

There is a moment of that frozen silence in which ice cubes could hibernate.

"Did you know that my main course of 'tiger prawns' is actually an anagram of my drink, 'spring water'?"

There. I'd said it. If it didn't fill her heart with glee, we could never have children.

"Really?"

Her face half lit up. It was a start, and perhaps we were going to be OK.

But all this nuttiness with words, and of seeing words in everything – how on earth did it all begin? And where on earth will it end?

Well, if you want to be a cryptic crossword setter, you'd better start thinking – unlike Henry VIII, who was a fat king – like a cryptic crossword setter.

For example, 'if I were you', immediately, as I write, suggests a possible letter replacement. For example, 'big' would be BUG, if I were U.

If I were you, I'd begin looking for words within words. But do you *really* want to be thinking like this? If so, read on, and take notes. If not, read on, and thank your lucky stars you listened to your parents.

HOW TO BECOME A CROSSWORD SETTER

Step one: Think like a crossword setter. See patterns (anagram of 'transept') in everything.

Step two: Win the lottery. Pick the correct numbers. I'd go for 1, 8, 15, 16, 28 and 34, but I've been wrong before. You will need at least 5 balls and the bonus ball in order to be able to put the time aside to practise crossword setting.

Step three: Lock yourself in a cupboard for at least a year, with a pen, a pad, and basic nutrients. Start writing clues. A tip would be, when you think you're good, you're probably still average. Keep practising until you consider yourself to be the best in the world. Balance your thoughts with your ego, and be realistic.

Step four: Get a proper job. Really, I would.

I didn't. I became a cryptic crossword setter.

MY STORY

I grew up in a village by the benign name of Forest Row, in the county of East Sussex, southern England.

Forest Row is a fairly safe place in which to grow up. The village had won Sussex's Best Kept Village Competition on more than one occasion – its hanging baskets were legendary. It had no night club, but two golf courses. John F. Kennedy once dropped by to visit its Catholic church while on his way to somewhere more important. On one occasion in my lifetime Forest Row made the national news on TV, albeit the travel information slot on a day of very severe road-works through the county.

My parents were hard-working Labour voters. They were happy to pay high income tax to subsidize those less privileged than themselves – that rare thing, the uncomplaining, and generous, success story.

My father had built from scratch a successful firm manufacturing plastic goods, my mum was a teacher, and together they worked tirelessly to give their four children a great start in life.

By the time I was seven we had moved to an imposing and remote pile on the outskirts of the village. We were very fortunate but, as is nearly always the case with kids, I for one certainly didn't fully appreciate how much effort our parents had made to get us there.

My father was a driven man, but difficult. Brilliantly practical, he could build replica veteran cars out of scrap metal and could turn his hand to fix or build pretty much anything. A dream of his had been to build an airship in the back garden. And, though he only ever got as far as the 'air' part of the 'airship', I know he could have done it.

However, much to my father's chagrin, his son proved more creative than practical. I saw myself as an artist: could sing; could write; couldn't change a fuse. My dad found my lack of common sense exasperating and the volcano would sometimes erupt.

I realize now he got angry and exasperated, because the words that gushed from the mountain weren't intended to reinforce my lack of self-belief, but occasionally they did, and in consequence I would often become withdrawn. Though I don't condone some of the things he said, he wanted me to succeed. He was frustrated in himself that he couldn't get me to achieve all the things he wanted for me, using methods that had worked for him. That passion and frustration could only have come from love, and a desire for me to do well.

And without my father I'm sure I wouldn't have loved wordplay. The family evening meal was rarely without a pun. Asking if I could get down from the table, he would respond with "No, you get down from a duck."

Even the food was sprinkled with verbal shimmies, the name of a particular favourite dessert (essentially a whipped milky pink thing) would alternate between 'pinky stuff' and 'stinky puff'.

We had a huge sprawling garden, at the perimeter of which were snaking paths in which I would wander alone through my teenage years, weaving mischief in my mind. My dad was a giant, and without him I wouldn't have been able to dream in superlatives, as I did.

But I also grew up scared. Scared of getting things wrong, scared of asking for things – scared that I would never be good enough not to be shouted at. In my head, I decided I had to be the best or else I would be vulnerable to verbal attack.

For my tenth birthday I was bought the *Guinness Book of World Records*. I became obsessed with the sorts of people in the book who would spend 12 years building a full-scale model of a passenger airliner out of matchsticks.

I wanted to be the next Steve Ovett, the British Olympic 800m champion and man of the people – a Sussex boy too. I asked myself how champions became champions. I decided they ran until they were sick. But then, how does one beat a champion? What could I do that they hadn't done? I decided I would run until I was sick, then rest briefly before running until sick again. Every night I would do this – for far, far too long – until I was forced to recognize my lack of talent, retiring from amateur solo middle-distance running at the age of 15.

So what next? I'd read in my *Book of World Records* that the fastest time for potting all 15 balls on an American pool table was 45 seconds. I practised around six hours a day for months and got it down to under a minute a few times. But I was no hustler.

Then it was the dream of becoming World Darts champion, pumping arrows into the dartboard in the shed at the bottom of the garden hour after hour – but I was Mr Inconsistent.

And then it happened that, in the early days of 1986, Halley's Comet was passing overhead, back for a brief flash across the heavens on its 76-year orbital journey around our solar system and beyond.

Hiding in my bedroom of an evening, as I would, I remember suddenly feeling compelled to ask my dad out onto the golf course adjacent to our home, to observe through his binoculars this hurtling body of light. For some reason, that night my fear of him briefly vanished.

The stroll, just a few words passing between us beneath a silent and sparkling sky, proved a stunning bonding experience, and beautiful.

Days later he was gone, in the blink of a heart attack, and things had changed forever – but I am still glad of that night.

My mother considered the best thing for me to do was to work at a bank. She meant well and I certainly needed a tremendous amount of guidance, for I had no appetite for the world of work. I spent two hellish years amusing myself by, while addressing envelopes, deliberately misspelling the names of their recipients to satisfy my juvenile sense of humour. Incidentally, a couple of years later I received a new credit card on which my name had been spelt HALPORN – coincidence? I think not.

I was a hopeless banker. So I landed a job at a pharmaceutical firm in East Grinstead. I would collect bags of urine from the local hospital, and considered myself the official piss-taker (a post I arguably still hold to this day).

But it was while working at this company, at the age of 21, that I lost my brother, Paul.

Paul had been my best friend. Growing up, we occupied adjacent bedrooms, his painted blue, mine red. But I would spend more time in his than in mine. We were both a little frightened of my dad, and what love seemed missing between father and sons was redeemed through our endless hours of chatter on football, The Beatles and ... actually I think that was the extent of it.

I never had the courage to tell him I loved him, though perhaps I didn't need to – and then it was suddenly too late.

Paul had left for Bradford University to study civil engineering, and we swapped letters weekly. Years passed, and we would see a little less of each other, but I like to think that bond was still there.

It was my brother's 27th birthday, and we received news of a car crash on the A5 in North Wales. The remainder of our family were driven the many hours from Sussex to Bangor, and we were with him at the end. I distinctly remember my mother trying to bring him out of the coma by reading crossword clues to him as he lay motionless on the life support system.

But the accident had proved too much, and after a long and emotional night he was gone. My father had died three years earlier, and now my brother. With my mum and my two sisters, I was the only male left. I began to believe I was next.

At 22, I left home to study maths and music at Canterbury, Kent. There is something about music and crosswords. I have heard there are players in the London Symphony Orchestra who, out of sight of the conductor, have a crossword upon their music stands during rehearsals. Several setters I know are musicians, and many solvers. Musicians and actors do a lot of sitting around, during rehearsals, and between takes.

And of course, Arthur Wynne himself was a musician. There is a natural rhythm and structure in music that also exists in the confines of a crossword grid.

I myself had aspired to being a composer as a youth. Magic could be created between barlines, as well as on a lattice of squares.

But I struggled. I had always had panic and anxiety attacks and believed I had no practical skills. With two bereavements fresh in my mind, the bottle beckoned. And I was fighting inner beliefs that I was stupid and useless, heading in the wrong direction, with my foot on the gas.

Until I discovered I could write crosswords.

I'd had no interest in my degree, in my second year turning up to only two lectures, mainly because I'd become so anxious I could hardly leave my home. I was probably going to end up leaving college a 26-year-old alcoholic with a third-class degree or worse. I just *had* to succeed in my quest to become a crossword setter.

But the standard of cryptic crosswords is so extraordinarily high in Britain. How would I ever make it? The big breakthrough for me happened one day in around 1992 when comparing what I considered to be the best two newspapers for crosswords, *The Times* and the *Guardian*. *The Times* perhaps edged it when it came to elegance, the *Guardian* for humour and invention.

There came my epiphany. What if I were to create a style that married the elegance of *The Times* with the *Guardian*'s humour?

I formulated a plan – to write just one puzzle that no one could turn down. I would rewrite it a thousand times if I had to, and then send it off to Araucaria.

Araucaria was my hero. Somehow, when I picked up an Araucaria puzzle, I felt loved, as if he wanted everything to be OK for you – and in my then turbulent state of mind, the thought of connecting with him was a godsend.

So, in my tiny box room at my student digs on Rhodaus Close, a few metres from Canterbury East train station, I set about practising writing clues.

In the same way that I'd run enough to have me be sick twice, I considered what would others do to become a crossword setter. In terms of time and effort, whatever a sane man would do, I would double it.

If a 'normal' setter would work nine to five, six days a week. I pledged to work seven days a week, from the moment of waking until the moment of sleep. I usually tell people it took a year, but thinking about this again, it was nearer three.

I took no phone calls, and soon the phone stopped ringing anyway. I wouldn't answer the door. I left the house only to visit the local petrol station to buy sandwiches and Diet Coke. My diet was appalling. My student housemates thought me mad – they did have a point. Hundreds of boxes had also been drawn all over the walls in my room.

Furthermore, I'd seen far too many public school references in crosswords for my liking, such as OB for Old Boy; and obscure Latin phrases abounded. It was an exclusive club, and I wanted the doors unlocked and flung open. How dare we keep all this fun to ourselves?

I resolved to bring in contemporary references. Let's not be snobs – most people have heard of Justin Bieber.

And a light sprinkling of smut might be in order, and could appeal to a younger audience – I was, of course, a student at the time.

I had to develop a style that the *Guardian* couldn't turn down. I had to pinpoint the secret of crossword comedy.

I had no choice. It was crosswords or madness and self-destruction. In my head I would probably never be capable of doing any other job in my life. And I was fighting that inner voice telling me I was incapable, and stupid, and that I had something wrong with my brain – a voice shared by many of us, I'm sure. If you have such thoughts, please don't listen to them, and be kind to yourself.

So finally, at the age of 26, I was ready.

Into a brown envelope marked 'Araucaria, c/o the *Guardian* Newspaper', I slipped one single honed-to-within-an-inch-of-its-life puzzle. The envelope was kissed and popped into the nearest post-box – and there began an excruciating wait.

I couldn't quite believe that the great man would write back, but write back he did. My whole future lay within that hallowed envelope. Then, hands a-tremble, it was open.

My eyes swam over his words, the gist of which was that he seemed to have enjoyed the puzzle and "if I liked, he would recommend me to the *Guardian*."

I don't like to think what would have happened had he never replied, or had he hated my puzzle; I had been in such a low place.

Everything was going to be all right.

And that hand-written letter by John Graham, aka Araucaria, now adorns my office wall, alongside the desk at which I set puzzles by 'Paul', the pseudonym I always intended to take for the *Guardian*, in honour of my brother, my best friend.

And these days I am married to a beautiful woman whose name is a one-word anagram of 'Entail', and we have a wonderful boy whose name appears in consecutive letters in 'caramel', 'taramasalata' and 'Bananarama'. His name is Aram.

Aram Paul.

Overleaf is that puzzle, and nearly two decades on, a few thoughts on it.

47. Set by Paul
The Guardian, April 19, 1995

ACROSS

8 Name sewn into footballers' underwear (8)

9 Actor – unknown featuring in 'Tearaway' (5)

10 One hears the Queen's off fish (4)

11 Time to join beer society going west, man – it's on the way (10)

12/3 Covering people in manure is sane ... (6,6)

14 ... Locking 'em inside with depression, insane (8)

15 An aid to one who's fuming, getting lost around hospital (3-4)

17 Eccentric return of stuttering Labour Party? (7)

20 To be wandering around alone is no longer useful (8)

22 Fairly attractive (6)

23 Wire broken in 22 across awful office equipment (10)

24 Pseudonym? One's not required – how sad (4)

25 Scottish town making appearance in the news (5)

26 Half admitted to large-scale pestilence (8)

DOWN

1 Rising Finnish (not Finish) river, one that's vast (8)

2 Came by a roundabout route to 24 down (4)

3 See 12 Across

4 With a leg either side, sit and read novel (7)

5 Still in bed, cold male shivering (8)

6 Within a board, reform ain't possible (10)

7 Rolls may be here (buns originally removed from trash) (6)

13 Disease producing frenzy (he got poorly, being injected) (10)

16 Bras aren't undone without somebody initially straying (8)

18 Libertine model adjusting hair in toilet (8)

19 Pagan girl overcome by passion (7)

21 Wild plant without flesh straddling rails (6)

22 Not quite finding a space for gingerbread (6)

24 Top secret monkey? (4)

First published in the *Guardian* newspaper.

Looking at it again, there are plenty of things I tried then that, 20 years later, are proving cringeworthy, although it's not a bad puzzle on the whole.

8 ac: Knickers. Says it all, really. Start as you mean to go on, I say.

9 ac: 'Actor' is loose for EXTRA, if not erroneous.

11 ac: 'it's on the way', loose again for TARMACADAM.

20 ac: would arguably be better as 'No longer useful to be wandering around alone (8)'

23 ac: nowadays I wouldn't use partial anagrams from another solution – it's a bit cheap.

1 dn: I had considered 'Finish' should appear with a capital 'F'. I'm less than sure now, and perhaps could have rewritten the clue.

7 and 13 dn: too much stuff in parentheses.

18 dn: model for T, so very hackneyed. Furthermore, the clue should read 'Libertine model with hair to adjust in toilet (8)'

As I say, I think it's not a bad effort, though on its publication I became immediately aware of the world of which I had just become a part – my first 'fan mail'.

It read as follows:

I am dismayed at the puzzle produced by your new setter Paul, particularly by its subject matter.

First we have 'knickers', later a girl being overcome by passion, the politically incorrect mental health issues at 11 and 12 across, the attack on stammerers at 17 across, some 'straddling', more filth at 16 down and a model in a toilet.

All I can say is, for those who follow the work of Paul, they are all:
Sad initially to be with American soldier on the way back (6,4)*

Yours sincerely,
Soapy Shaft-Twiglets

[the gentleman's name has been anagrammatically disguised]

*Sexist gits

I had entered the mysterious world of the cryptic crossword, but hadn't accounted for the underworld of cryptic crossword solvers. My life would never be the same again.

So, we have learned how to become a setter, but once there, what is the process behind writing a crossword? Here we shall look at, specifically, the cryptic crossword, but many of the thought processes are similar for other types of crossword.

HOW TO WRITE A (CRYPTIC) CROSSWORD

It all starts with an idea.

Aside from my freelance work as a cryptic crossword setter for various newspapers, I edit a magazine called *Crossword Mix* for Puzzler Media Ltd (PML), the UK's leading puzzle magazine publishers. The office in which I work (infrequently!) is a chapel of serenity. Word lovers at PML heads down, are lost in their worlds of kriss-kross, wordsearch and Sudoku.

My wordplay-loving colleague Roger Prebble shuffles over to my desk. "Here's a good one," he says. "Presbyterians. It's an anagram of someone famous."

I'd love to be able to tell you I worked it out. I didn't. That pause for thought was soon interrupted, Roger being too eager to let me know, rather than let me think.

"It's BRITNEY SPEARS," he sniggers, his heaving shoulders lifting a broad smile high onto his beaming face. Roger has been in the puzzle business for many decades but on discovering a fun, or perhaps juvenile, piece of wordplay, he returns instantly to being a little boy.

"Wow, can I steal it?" I ask. "Is that one of yours?"

Ownership of a clue or of an idea is a moot point. Crossword setters may write the same clue independent of one another.

In this case, it doesn't take long to hone the idea. It will be a puzzle about Britney Spears, but dressed up as a puzzle about Presbyterians and given a religious feel. Then, as the solver undoes the crossword word by word, there shall be a moment in which the references to one particular answer, seemingly related to Presbyterianism, suddenly reveal themselves to be referring to the classic works of the US no-longer-teen pop sensation, such as 'Oops!... I Did It Again' and 'Baby One More Time'.

I shall create that moment of bathos, the descent from the exalted to the banal, where both the penny, and the level of erudition required, drop. But to have the solver get the punch line of the puzzle at the right moment, the setter must understand how the solver is to solve the puzzle. The solving of the religious clues should ideally happen first.

We crossword setters are sneaky devils indeed, and if we know what we are doing, an easily solved clue with a 'Z' in the answer, for example, will probably encourage the solver to look at clues whose solutions sit around that particular area of the puzzle in which now sits the word with the 'Z', and not look yet at the part of the puzzle in which is the punch line. After years of experience, I can usually tell, more or less, the order in which the solver will fill the grid.

Not everyone approves of a Britney Spears puzzle. However, I think contemporary culture is vital (and fun) if we are to keep the game of puzzle solving fresh.

Every puzzle, as I say, starts with an idea. Sometimes I pop an idea onto my un-cryptically titled 'New Ideas' Word document, and when I've got around five or six (often half-formed clues), I find a grid with suitable word lengths to suit that puzzle.

Here are a few thoughts I've had over the years as I've been puzzle solving. There are some lovely coincidences, and other moments where the setter is pleasantly surprised by the outcome of a clue.

For example, I'd filled in a particular *Guardian* puzzle with two consecutive 15-letter entries down the middle reading NATIONAL LOTTERY and RUSSIAN ROULETTE. If I can't think of a clue straight away for these long entries, often they get left until last. It was only at the end of the setting process that I realized the latter solution could be defined by the former. And so, the clue for RUSSIAN ROULETTE became 'National lottery where the *last* thing you'll do is lose! (7,8)'.

On another occasion I'd written every clue in a puzzle only to be left with T_S_I_G. Hmmm, TESTING, TASTING or TOSSING? Well, TOSSING jumped out at me, but experience told me that *–ing* words are hard to clue. TOSSING is *sot* backwards, then *sing*. Still nothing occurred as an idea. It was only then that I noticed the word TANG around the outside in 'TA(*sti*)NG.' And TANG means 'flavour'. This is exactly the sort of coincidence we are looking for – a sort of masked serendipity. It's our job as cryptic crossword setters to find what's already there, and sometimes it is a happy coincidence indeed. So, I have TANG. 'ITS' is hidden backwards inside it. Experience tells me I am on to something good. It is only a short step
later that I am left with the &Lit-type clue 'It's about passing flavour around (7)'. Cryptic, but straight too.

In the 1990s, Girl Power was sweeping the nation, and I got caught up in it, creating a Spice Girls puzzle, in which BABY, SCARY, POSH, GINGER and SPORTY, along with SPICE were all entries. By chance, the long entry down the middle of this grid was THE ETON WALL GAME, a bruising public school free-for-all supposedly played by young gentlemen. Some might argue it is simply an excuse for a mass brawl.

But how was I to clue this? Well, what can one say about it? Well, it's posh. Aha, suddenly an unexpected link to the theme. A moment later I realized two more of her 'singing' colleagues are also implicated, and the clue became: 'It's Posh, Sporty and a little bit Scary (3,4,4,4)'.

Back to my New Ideas list. It currently contains words and phrases including:

Cherokee – because a native American was previously referred to as a brave, and the word 'hero' (someone brave) is hidden within the word (CHEROkee).
Will you marry me? – simply because it starts with 'willy'. How juvenile!
Gigaflop – because I love the word, and because it conjures up an image of a disastrous concert.
Gardyloo – a word cried by the Scots once, in warning to pedestrians below that slops were about to be thrown onto the street – because that's fun too. And:
Much Ado about Nothing – it occurred to me, and I can't remember how (!) that the OTHI in the 'NOTHING' of 'Much Ado About Nothing' is (very arguably) equal to OTHELLO. OT = OT, and HI = HELLO. There's something in there, but it's a fine line between being clever, and forcing a Shakespearean connection out of the word. Might I be crossing that line? Perhaps that's why this idea has been on my 'New Ideas' list for a couple of years …

Sometimes a single idea gives birth to a puzzle. Here's one such example, as we go through the process of creating a crossword:

Step 1. Get an idea
Find a word, a group of words, a theme that excites you, and with which you can see you can create something fun. Here's my idea:

Teenage Mutant Ninja Turtles.

Why does this excite me? Because it's (arguably!) fun, and because considering who the turtles are, namely Leonardo, Michelangelo, etc, this seems the perfect opportunity to create something with a body swerve, where the solver thinks they've ordered the Teriyaki grilled poussin, only to be served up a chicken bargain bucket.

Remember, this is just my thinking on this particular puzzle, which has a bit of a twist. If you are creating your own puzzle – do feel free to have a go, as it's great fun – simply choose a few words or phrases you like and start from there.

So, back to creating this particular puzzle.

I shall note down all the words needed here. I'm already starting to think about how to load the grid up in such a way to seem like we are dealing with high art. What if I were to include some of the paintings by these masters? Let's list some, creating a longer word list, before I shorten it again to the most important solutions, and to those entries with an interesting word structure:

Furthermore, I shall write the word lengths beside the words – you'll see why later.

Here's my list (preferably ensuring all entries are well-known – always avoid obscurities if you can help it – it's not about you showing off what you know):

TEENAGE MUTANT NINJA TURTLES (7,6,5,7)
LEONARDO (8)
MICHELANGELO (12)
RAPHAEL (7)
DONATELLO (9)
MONA LISA (4,4)
THE SCHOOL OF ATHENS (3,6,2,6)
THE LAST SUPPER (3,4,6)
CREATION OF ADAM (8,2,4)
DAVID (5)
THE LAST JUDGMENT (3,4,8)
SISTINE CHAPEL (7,6)
ADORATION OF THE MAGI (9,2,3,4)

Hang on, but some of these are really long answers, and we only have a 15×15 grid to play with. What are we actually out to achieve here, and how much can we fit into the grid?

In general, with thematic puzzles (most puzzles aren't thematic) we can fit around 12 or 13 shortish entries into the grid. With longer entries, it could be as few as four or five.

So we don't have much room. So what are the entries that just *have* to appear in this puzzle?

TEENAGE MUTANT NINJA TURTLES (the punch line)

All four of the artists? Hmm, perhaps not possible, especially if I am to include Michelangelo, meaning I have to use a grid with 12-letter entries. What if I just use one famous artist and his paintings? After all, people have heard of *Mona Lisa* and *The Last Supper*. Shall we just stick with LEONARDO, and hopefully fit in two or three, or perhaps four, of his most famous works?

And if so, which ones? What are the criteria?

I need to consider how I might write the clue. There are a number of different types of clue (see Section 2, Chapter 5). In the rudimentary sense of simply classifying how one might go about writing the clues, we can choose words that would end up producing some enjoyment for the solver. Thinking this far ahead before even filling the grid makes for a puzzle that ends up being more fun.

THE LAST SUPPER
MONA LISA
ADORATION OF THE MAGI

These seem fairly well-known, to varying extents. So is there scope for good clues in these entries? Perhaps Mona Lisa could be a HIDDEN type of clue, 'Somewhat horMONAL IS, Art by LEONARDO'. Hey, that's not bad.

We should always have balance in a cryptic puzzle – not too many of one particular type of clue.

Can I see something in THE LAST SUPPER? An anagram plus UPPER at the end? SALE backwards in an anagram?

And what about ADORATION OF THE MAGI? It's got 'oration' in there. And what else? Actually, it says 'oration of them' in the middle, which could be 'their speech?' I like that. OK, so I've decided to find a grid that fits (with word lengths):

TEENAGE MUTANT NINJA TURTLES (7,6,5,7)
LEONARDO (8)
ADORATION OF THE MAGI (9,2,3,4)
THE LAST SUPPER (3,4,6)
MONA LISA (4,4)

And then we can find other words that fit the grid, as we go along ...

Step 2. Find a crossword grid that fits those words – or create one.
Newspapers around the world have varying policies on grids. For example, see rules for the *New York Times* later in this book, where constructors create their own grids.

In Britain, for the *Guardian*, *The Times* and the *Daily Telegraph* all have lists of numbered grids from which the setter must make a selection. For the *Financial Times* and the *Independent*, we can create our own grids. On average each paper has around 60 different grids on its database.

When submitting our puzzles, we let the crossword editors know which number grid we've used, and that grid pattern from that paper's crossword database can be pasted straight onto the page.

I plan to write this for the *Guardian,* so look for a grid with entries of 4,5,6,7,8 and 9 letters. That should cover everything.

In the olden days (pre-2000?), we had printouts of all the grids, and used to tap all the clues out onto an A4 sheet of paper, then print out a sheet of grids, and with a pair of scissors cut round the appropriate one, fill in the grid with biro and then staple it to the top left-hand side of the A4 sheet, before popping the puzzle in the snail mail to the editor for consideration!

Nowadays all crossword setters use computer software to help create their puzzles, and to submit them. I use a piece of software called Crossword Compiler, which is the preferred software for setters in the UK, and also away from these shores, for example in the *New York Times*.

Once I have chosen my grid – in this case *Guardian* grid 61* seems to do the trick – we can begin the really fun bit!

Grid 61 is already on my Crossword Compiler software database, so I open it up and look at the empty grid.

*This may come across as a little bit sad, but I can usually recognize the number of the grid used in a particular day's newspaper at a glance – a note to the socially inadequate, it is ill-advised to point out to commuters that the puzzle they are solving is on *Guardian* grid 61. It is my experience that with this opening gambit friendships are rarely kindled.

Step 3. Fill the grid with words
We're now looking at a logic problem. Sometimes we have words in our list with letters on which we should be keeping an eye.

For example, a 'Z' or a 'J' if put in the wrong place can cause immediate problems in the grid-filling process. For example, if we were to put a word beginning with 'J' at 19 across, that would leave us with a word at 6 down ending in 'J', leaving me only with a few options such as the towns of BEGAMGANJ (in India), KARIMGANJ (in India also) and SOVOBODNYJ, which is an alternative spelling for a town in Russia. That seems obvious, but a 'J' absolutely anywhere in a square intersecting with another solution can bring the setter to a halt.

Of course, in this whole process, we are talking about British grids, often those used in countries of the commonwealth, such as Australia and South Africa. Crucially, we are not here talking about American-style grids, the direct descendants of Arthur Wynne's closely interlocking puzzle of 1913. In the US, the filling process is a whole new ball game, as American football is to British football (or soccer): a more bruising encounter, with huddles and shoulder-pads, as the words mesh and grind; not necessarily pretty to watch, but an opportunity for some pretty quick thinking in the construction process, and to be several steps ahead with your game plan.

Back to Britain, and this grid.

The Crossword Compiler database has lists of all the available words for a particular space (for example an eight-letter-long space), and we can choose any one of them.

So, do we want these Indian or Russian towns in our puzzle? An Indian themed puzzle, or Russian perhaps, might be perfect. But for a generally British market (although the *Guardian* is certainly read all over the world), let's stick with stuff we know.

In our word list, we don't really have any awkward letters, save for the 'J' in NINJA, but if you look at the possible positions for NINJA at 1 down, 3 down, 22 down or 23 down, the 'J' will always be safely tucked away in a square not intersecting with any other words – where it does intersect we call this a checking letter – and it's therefore not causing a problem. Non-checking letters, such as the 'J', we call 'un-checked letters', or sometimes in crossword jargon 'unches'.

So, I set about filling in my grid, noticing which letters cross where. ADORATION, for example, looks good for 13 down, as the checked letters are A, O, A, I and N, giving us lots of options for across entries going the other way. TURTLES looks good for 4 down, where the 'L' is the start of an 8-letter word, and we can enter LEONARDO at 11 across. And so on – simply a logic problem, and so much fun. I'd recommend you buy the software, and start to write your own crosswords, then send them to friends for birthdays. You could put words in the grid that mean something to the recipient – a really personal gift.

As we progress with the grid fill, we keep pressing the 'Autofill' button, and the computer gives us options for the rest of the puzzle.

Furthermore, at any stage, we can also check all the possibilities for a particular entry. If we have H_R_ _ for a particular word, we can select 'Autofind' from the drop-down menu, and find all the words on the database with this pattern. In this case, they are:

HARDY, HARED, HAREM, HARKS, HARMS, HARPY, HARRY, HARSH, HARTS, HERBS, HERBY, HERDS, HEROD, HERON, HERTZ, HIRED, HIRER, HIRES, HORAL, HORDE, HORNS, HORNY, HORST, HORSY, HORUS, HURLS, HURON, HURRY, HURST, HURTS, HYRAX.

Some words may appeal more than others. Which would you choose?

So we keep going until the grid is filled, selecting options from those available, and considering all the time how we might write a clue for our chosen words.

Step 4. Write the clues

I shan't take you through the process for all the clues in this puzzle (for the book is too short!) but very briefly, in writing cryptic crossword clues we are simply looking for:

1 A definition in each clue
and
2 A cryptic part (sometimes called the 'wordplay').

The thinking behind every clue differs, but as long as the clue makes some sort of sense when you read it, and doesn't look like a load of random words piled together, you have a cryptic crossword clue.
I love the process. Here's a recent thought of mine.

Considering how to write a clue for RICHARD III, I first asked myself, "What do I know about him?"

Well, at the time of writing, the fifteenth-century monarch, who reigned over England until his death in 1485 at the Battle of Bosworth Field, was hot news. His body had just been found underneath a car park in Leicester.

As crossword setters, we are always looking for links in wordplay. The car park link seemed something I could exploit for humour. But how?

And suddenly I realized that the king was found in the word 'parKING'. Better still, he was found 'buried' in 'parKING lot!' Now we were getting somewhere. But how could a cryptic clue be written that made sense? Well, we have PAR/KING/ LOT. Perhaps I could write the clue as a charade, defining each of those three parts of the solution. What seems interesting suddenly is that LOT is another word for 'fate'. And now we have RICHARD III = king meeting LOT = fate. PAR means average, as in the (supposedly!) average score on a golf hole. So, 'Where the average Richard III has met fate (7,3)': PAR/KING/ LOT. This is all wordplay, and perhaps good enough not to need a further definition.

But wait, something else can be seen in PAR/KING/ LOT.

On the outside of the ten letters we can see a very helpful four-letter word – P(arking) LOT, 'plot'. A plot is a grave! Now I'm getting really excited! But what does that leave us with, after the elements describing Richard III and the grave? We have: P(AR/KING) LOT. AR: quite beautifully, in cryptic crosswords R = KING, as in the Latin REX. So if R can also be a king, we could finish off the clue like this: 'Grave in which a sovereign, Richard III, found buried? (7,3)': P(A/R/KING) LOT.

And that's the process of writing a clue, though it doesn't have to be as complex for you!

Clues written, I usually provide explanations of all clues and email the puzzle to the relevant editor. The finished Teenage Mutant Ninja Turtles puzzle, with clues and explanations, is overleaf. Different editors request their own system for titles. Hugh at the *Guardian* would have received this from me as G61PaulAntenatal, where G= *Guardian*, 61 is the grid number, then my pseudonym, then the answer to the first clue.

Key for explanations below: * = anagram, < = reversed, letters in lower case are those deleted

Across: 1 AN/TE(NAT<)AL, **6** TO GO, **8** T(AVER)NER<, **9** FO(ET)AL, **10** N(EVAD)A< Dave referring to David, **11** L(EON*)ARDO(n), **12** C/A</STRO*, **15** S(to)KE/LET ON, **16** GOL/(GOT/H)A<, **21** C(AS)EMENT, **24** T/IRAN/A &LIT, **25** M(ON)A LI/SA<, **26** (b) ONCE, **27** IN TEST/(p)ACY.

Down: 1 AD AGE?, **2/19** THE LAST S*/UPPER, **5** L(EFT)OVERS, **6/22A/3/4** ANAG Leonardo, Raphael, Donatello and Michaelangelo (sic) on film and small screen in the 1980s, and recently making a comeback, **7** ANAG GOES RAIN D, **13/14** AD(ORATION/ OF THE M)AGI(o), **17** ANAG DANGER + PINEAPPLE (without PIN and APPLE, i.e. only with E)&LIT, **18** AT/TEMPT, **20** PA(T)ELLA, **22** ANAG, **23** HIDDEN.

48. The Finished Puzzle
By John Halpern, aka Paul

ACROSS

1 Before little one emerges, an aquatic bird shelters brown back (9)
6 Nation for sale? (4)
8 Landlord has to declare in retrieval of payment (8)
9 Strange being inside baby animal, as it is unborn (6)
10 Casually named work of Michelangelo (?) in an inverted state (6)
11 Bacon not entirely accepts one freaky artist! (8)
12 A Cuban leader retired, revolutionary sort? (6)
15 City team doesn't have to reveal supporter (8)
16 Calvary became hot in recollection of a diary (8)
19 See 2 Down
21 Stick outside as window frame (8)
22 See 6 Down
24 Capital of the country, capital of Albania (6)
25 11's nation holds on while in recession (4,4)
26 Head scalped in days gone by (4)
27 Where international cricketers play fast having lost opener, no will here (9)

DOWN

1 Saw the era of Saatchi & Saatchi? (5)
2/19 11's wasted less with that part of a shoe (3,4,6)
3 See 6
4 See 6
5 *Romeo and Juliet* gobbling newt – what remains? (9)
6/22A/3/4 11 was one of those extraordinary men, just genuine talent at art (7,6,5,7)
7 August goes with rain, Scotland ultimately stormy (9)
13/14 11's delivery theirs, in short movement (9,2,3,4)
17 Potential danger with pineapple, pin being pulled and fruit going off? (7)
18 Go towards to lead astray (7)
20 Bone specialist finally placed in dish (7)
22 Sign in sum, dashed? (5)
23 Mean to get some protection, as tyrant (5)

First published in the *Guardian* newspaper.

CHAPTER 9
SOLVING CHAMPIONSHIPS AND CHAMPIONS

I made the mistake of once suggesting to Richard Browne, *The Times* crossword editor, that we bring a little pizzazz to the event of the *Times* Crossword Championships. Perhaps 'pizzazz' had been a leap too far. The Championships do not have the glitz of the US Puzzle Tournament, though I do recall some glamorous heats at London's Alexandra Palace a few years back where, under otherwise strict exam conditions, the papers were collected by hired beauties in bikinis and stilettos. In retrospect, where concentration and focus are prerequisites for success, this was probably an ill-advised distraction.

In 1970, the inaugural year of the championships, around 20,000 people completed the first stage of the tournament, which was to provide a correct solution to any one of five puzzles printed in May. Three further eliminator puzzles were employed, the third of which was so difficult that only 42 correct solutions were received. These were ignored, and the 300 or so who solved Puzzle 2 correctly were invited to the first tournament proper.

The finals, from the outset to this day, were to take place over two days. Day One in 1970 saw a series of eight puzzles attempted, with 36 competitors invited back for Day Two, and another four puzzles. The winner was Roy Dean, a Foreign Office diplomat, later to become a *Times* crossword setter himself.

Prize-wise, a variety of sponsors have provided cash, on one occasion a car with a crossword on its roof, and on a further occasion (with sponsors Inter-City Trains in 1992) a national railcard for the year, providing an opportunity for the then youngest-ever winner, Guy Haslam, to travel to every football game played that season by his beloved Aston Villa.

In my experience, the setters of British cryptic crosswords with whom I hang around tend to make undistinguished solvers. More often than not, I don't finish a puzzle. Araucaria himself claims to be an average solver, but Enigmatist is a different kettle of fish, as a previous *Times* Crossword Champion in 1996.

According to the online Unofficial *Times* Crossword Championship page, run by former champion Peter Biddlecombe, around 80 per cent of competitors are male. He says the best explanation he can give for this is that most solvers are commuters. The average age is 50, and most are educated to postgraduate level. Most work in offices, laboratories or educational institutions. Programmers, mathematicians and scientists seem to be more successful than those who work with words, such as writers, translators and professors of English Literature.

Winners through the years include a school headmaster, a lecturer in Russian and Slavonic Studies, a doctor, a maths teacher, and a computer systems designer and programmer.

MARK GOODLIFFE

Mark Goodliffe, *Times* Crossword Champion for the last five years running, is a solving machine. Editor Richard Browne says that at the last tournament, in the time between his completing the three final puzzles and the runner-up finishing, Mark reached down into his bag, pulled out that day's Jumbo crossword, and polished that off too.

"Once I have some letters in the grid," says Mark, "I'm very prone to focus on pattern recognition."

"I doubt that I am much better as a cold-solver than many others. I also think I've trained myself a bit not to go through the same processes again and again for a clue I'm struggling with, which may save time. I don't really agree with the people who say that speedy solvers get less enjoyment from a puzzle than others, as I presume we all have exactly the same number of 'aha' moments – those who are quick just have fewer of the other, unsuccessful thoughts.

"I describe my general knowledge as 'very wide and very shallow' – I know the names but not the plots from lots of plays and novels, can reel off lists of capital cities I've never visited, and always wonder if a programme like *Newsnight Review* is a joke, as I find it so hard to believe anyone would have such deep knowledge of literature, etc.

"I've never felt my job as a finance director is relevant, except inasmuch as I have less time for solving than I'd like – though perhaps I'd have spent that time on Sudoku instead! I am always surprised how often the best solvers are musicians or theoretical mathematicians – I'm certainly neither."

THE AMERICAN CROSSWORD PUZZLE TOURNAMENT

As far back as the 1920s, the *New York Herald Tribune* began to stage crossword contents where champion puzzle gladiators would solve huge puzzles in the Waldorf Astoria, apparently with thousands of puzzle fans in attendance. And it's still going on today. Currently staged annually at a hotel in Brooklyn, The American Crossword Puzzle Tournament (ACPT) is described on Crosswordtournament.com as follows:

"Directed by *New York Times* Crossword Puzzle Editor Will Shortz, this is the nation's oldest and largest crossword competition. Solvers tackle eight original crosswords created and edited specially for this event. Scoring is based on accuracy and speed. Prizes are awarded in more than 20 categories, including a $5,000 grand prize. Evening games, guest speakers, and a wine and cheese reception allow solvers to meet each other in a relaxed and entertaining atmosphere."

At the 2013 tournament, special events included eight Arthur Wynne puzzles from the *New York World*. Playoff commentary on the tournament was provided by Greg Pliska, host of *A Way With Words*, a radio show about words and language broadcast on many NPR stations, and featuring Will Shortz, and comedian Ophira Eisenberg, host of NPR's *Ask Me Another*.

Fun and terrifying in equal measure, those who have seen the hugely entertaining and highly recommended 2006 film *Wordplay*, based upon the tournament and its pencil-chewing heroes, will be familiar with it as a glorious snapshot of all that is wonderful about word lovers, a nerdfest of obsessives.

But, though many solve, few are destined to become champions. Here we meet the top three finishers at the 2013 tournament.

DAN FEYER (WINNER, 2010–13)

So which came first, the champion crossword solver or the boiled egg? It might well be a close-run thing. Dan Feyer, a professional pianist having majored in music at Princeton, finishes the *New York Times* crossword in an average of three-and-a-half minutes.

The championship round of the ACPT is an exciting, edge-of-your-seat activity. Three sets of three finalists solve increasingly difficult puzzles in front of a ballroom full of competitors and friends. The contestants use dry-erase markers on large whiteboards, and listen to white noise on iPods so that they can't hear the live commentary.

Dan describes the final moments of the ACPT:

"We're led into the grand ballroom, walking past the seven or eight hundred cheering spectators, and up onto a small stage with the three large empty grids mounted on easels. The white noise is rather soothing, and helps to calm the nerves that have inevitably started to jangle. When an official taps me on the shoulder (because I can't hear the word 'Begin'), I begin to scan the printed crossword in my left hand for a clue that I can answer. In a crossword this hard, that can take a while.

"Up until now, I've been up on that stage at six consecutive tournaments, moving up from the C Division (where the clues are comparable to a Wednesday or Thursday *New York Times* puzzle) to the B Division (a Friday or Saturday puzzle, the hardest of the week) and finally the A Division, whose championship puzzle is trickier than any that's regularly published in the United States. Due to my experience as a professional musician, I don't get nervous performing in front of a crowd, which might be an advantage over my rivals. But it's hard not to be tense when you're sequestered with the other finalists in a hotel meeting room for 30–40 minutes.

"The rest of the tournament is based on speed solving, and every lost second could make a difference. In the finals, I try to be more deliberate and not rush into a fatal mistake. As I finish the puzzle, I double-check that all the squares are filled, and call 'done!'. The crowd erupts in cheers, which are loud enough to be heard through the iPods and bulky headphones. Or so I'm told – so far, I've always finished first."

ANNE ERDMANN (SECOND IN 2013)
Anne is a regular podium finisher in the ACPT.
"I think you have to have some kind of a love of words, which can take a lot of different forms – a love of reading or writing, for example, or a love for puns and wordplay. An enjoyment of logic and order is also helpful, as crosswords follow various rules and patterns. I myself have a drive for completion, not just in solving puzzles, but in my life – I would have made a great civil servant whose job it was to do nothing but fill out forms all day! When I see little empty white boxes, I want to fill them!"

Describe the experience of your participation in the ACPT?
"I always laugh when I head off to New York to compete in the ACPT every year, for which I take a couple of vacation days from work, and my colleagues say things like 'Have fun!' The ACPT is many things to me, but 'fun' isn't the first word that comes to mind. It's very difficult to make the A finals, because of the number of top solvers who are capable of doing so. I tell people to think of it as our Olympics, and it brings with it the associated tensions and stresses, for me at least. Don't get me wrong, I love seeing the people there, most of whom I only get to see once a year, and I enjoy the various non-competition puzzles and events, but, it's still an intense experience overall, and sometimes I wonder why I keep putting myself through it!"

You must know a lot of wacky words, and obscure stuff?
Like Tyler, and given the nature of the closely-interlocking words in an American-style grid, Anne observes: "You can find lists of 'crosswordese' in a lot of different sources, and I'd refer you to one of those. Most of those words I learned by osmosis very early on in my solving career. Right now my focus is on expanding my pop-culture vocabulary – I have no interest in watching TV, going to movies, or reading celebrity magazines, and as a result I have huge knowledge gaps in that area, especially regarding celebrity names, which can be pretty wackily spelled! (I haven't quite forgiven the Brits for the Spice Girls – so many of them with such cutesy little names to memorize, sigh ...)"

TYLER HINMAN (THIRD IN 2013)
A games developer and software engineer, Tyler was American Crossword Puzzle Tournament Champion five years running, 2005–09 (but finished third in 2013). I asked him what it is that makes a champion solver. The answer is perhaps unsurprising.

"It's practice, really. That's how I got good.

"The best solvers tend to be musicians and math/computer people.

"Both of those realms involve rapidly digesting and interpreting coded information (e.g. musical notes or computer code), much like the odd, abbreviated language of a crossword clue."

Tyler, like many top solvers, says he has no wish to cure his obsession.

"I'll frequently rewrite a letter if I don't think it's neat enough (though not in a tournament, of course). And I have a folder called 'To Be Solved' on my desktop, where I ritualistically download the day's puzzles. Why would I want to cure it?'

And all this practice means Tyler has become a quick solver. I mean, really quick.

"Taking the Monday *NYT* puzzle, I can do it on the computer in about 1:30 and on paper in about 2:30. I think I got a 2:06 out of it once. That was several years ago; I don't speed-solve that much on paper. I don't really enjoy it."

You wouldn't think at that rate of solving that crossword champions have time to reflect on the clues. But it seems even at speed there is always a part of the brain with an opinion.

"Crosswords should reflect how people speak, which excludes a lot of 'crosswordese'. Tough trivia and vocabulary can be fine, but if you have two toughies crossing each other, many solvers will cry foul; there's nothing more irritating than having one blank square you can't fill."

MARK GOODLIFFE IN THE ACPT

UK champ Mark's solving talents stretch further than the shores of Britain. The ACPT in both 2012 and 2013 featured a US vs UK cryptic challenge, a sort of Ryder Cup of crosswords – but with the UK instead of Europe and with just two players – and presumably without whooping. OK, so not quite like the Ryder Cup.

The leading American cryptic solver Anne Erdmann and Mark Goodliffe completed their cryptic puzzle in respectively the wrong and the right side of four minutes.

Although the puzzle had been compiled by the American Rich Silvestri, Mark admits, "Of course us Brits have a considerable advantage with the cryptic puzzles.'"

Mark was also delighted to take 246th place in the main event, providing "a chance for me to look at the best solvers the way others look at me solving cryptic crosswords."

THE FASTEST OFFICIAL SOLVE

On December 19, 1970, Foreign Office diplomat Roy Dean turned up on BBC Radio's *Today* programme for a chat about crosswords, and his ability to solve them in double-quick time – he had just won the inaugural *Times* Crossword Championships. Suddenly, live on air, a challenge was thrust upon him. Handed that day's *Times* crossword and a pen, a stopwatch was activated: 3 minutes 45 seconds later, and the puzzle was complete.

The Guinness Book of Records still records this as the fastest-solved *Times* cryptic crossword under test conditions.

CHAPTER 10
THE CROSSWORD EDITORS

Crossword setters and constructors are a funny lot. So, frankly, we need our editors.

Without naming names – though I am tempted – many of us are difficult sods, and sometimes in the heat of a mixed metaphor our creative juices overflow and we blow a fuse. In fact, I once threw a kipper at an editor (or was it a meatball, or was it at a nun? Either I forget or it was a fantasy ...).

I have yet to meet a crossword editor who is not a total delight. Yes, I would say that, wouldn't I? One is aware on which side of the bread one's butter sits. However, it seems toe-curlingly true.

Anyhow, enter the crossword editor. Many newspapers of worth will have one, many of non-worth too. But what on earth is a crossword editor? What do they do? How did they get into this seemingly most arcane of professions – and how does one sneak things past them?

Let's begin by comparing the US with the UK:

The USA: populism, pizzazz and punnery
Stanley Newman

A passionate delight, and a character among men of letters, Stan Newman is never short of words.

A native of Brooklyn, the winner of the inaugural US Open Crossword Championship, and of the American Crossword Puzzle Tournament (1982), Stan is long-time editor of the nationally syndicated *Newsday* Crossword. And he's not shy to dub himself the CEO of Crosswords.

"Puzzles should be generationally balanced in subject matter, their difficulty coming from devious wordplay, rather than from obscurity or general knowledge," he says.

"There shouldn't be any 'you either know it or you don't' clues. General knowledge should go no further than 'Capital of Italy'."

Stan quotes a recent clue of his: "Argentina's daily football newspaper (3), answer: OLÉ."

"Although you probably wouldn't have the general knowledge to get there," he argues, "OLÉ just makes sense, doesn't it? That clue is surely more interesting than 'Spanish exclamation'."

Stan 'declared war' on the *New York Times* crossword in the 1980s. He saw it as being both disdainful and ignorant of the modern world and too reliant on obscurities. He was to set himself up as a crossword crusader, a militant, and the foremost populist among a network of squares. However, he is the first to admit he is never going to please all of the people all of the time.

"Readers get quite intense," he says.

"'How dare you spell the word "enure" – it is "inure"!'"

"I find the level of high dudgeon in the email is usually in direct proportion to how wrong they are. But despite some solvers' ignorance, I *usually* respond with kindness."

Over the years, Stan has been a standard-bearer for the art, ensuring crosswords are both current and flowing with the current.

"While still the chief method by which people access their crosswords is through the newspapers, you have to keep going to wherever your audience is going. There is a fair amount of migration to the most popular delivery mechanisms – Facebook, for example."

But whether quick or cryptic, across the world crossword-compiling software is now standard for setters of puzzles. Grid-filling can happen at the press of a button, but it is still very much down to the setter to choose words that work, and to write clues that fit those words.

Stan says this has really helped.

"I certainly make far better crosswords than I did when I learned it with just a pencil and a large eraser" [he smiles].

Stan's continued contribution to the world of crosswords and his undying battle against obscurity and for accessibility has been a major factor in bringing wordplay to the masses.

And with around 50 million crossword solvers from Alabama to Wyoming, the populist has played no small part in guaranteeing the popularity of crosswords across the United States.

Britain – quintessential quirks and quips
Hugh Stephenson

"I get about 20 letters a day, mostly abusive. I think it's human nature – people generally write in only to complain. Mental health people are particularly dreadful. They complain about 'bananas' or 'nuts' being an anagram indicator. That's madness."

Jovial and approachable, Hugh Stephenson is the editor of the quick and cryptic crosswords in the UK's *Guardian* newspaper.

"The Zionists are difficult, and I also get people arguing that IRA should not be defined as 'Terrorists', but as 'Freedom-fighters'. And then there are the 'sisters'. Feminists can be a nuisance."

It seems the word 'tart' seems to pose a particular problem in the *Guardian*.

"A recent clue 'Good girls, or tarts (5,2,6)'* is very nice, I think you'll agree. But the sisters would beg to differ."

*MAIDS OF HONOUR

And then there's this particular favourite from Hugh's postbag, which shouts:

"And how many times has this happened already? And how many times have you made pathetic excuses and tried to shuffle the blame off onto someone else? You, sir, are unfit to run a whelk stall! Stand down, please, and let someone with more clout, more guts, more pride and more self-respect take over."

There are also more personal exchanges, Hugh continues.

"I am the recipient of constant gifts and letters from nutcases and stalkers. A particular pest has been after me for a while. "'Why are you ignoring me?' she wails. 'We can take the ferry from Newhaven and run away to France, you know.'"

Then there are the crosswords. An editor's daily routine, of course, means dealing with crossword setters.

"There are one or two prima donnas, some arguably with justification, as they are very good at what they do. But if they keep on being difficult, I can always choose to withdraw their puzzle. It is the youngsters who are often very precious about their work. When I respond with 'It's only a crossword, you know', it doesn't seem to go down too well."

The quick crosswords are set by a team of three compilers, on a rotational basis of three weeks on, six weeks off; the cryptic crosswords by a team of about 20, only one of whom is a woman. Asked why it's generally men who become crossword setters, Hugh has a quick response.

"Asperger's, perhaps?"

I think I know what Hugh means. We men are totally fascinated by something like the structure of an array of squares, its interconnecting cogs and wheels. When filling in a grid, a naked Beyoncé on a bed of marshmallows could float past my window, and an eyelid I would not bat.

Like Stan Newman, across the page and across the Pond, Hugh is quick to realize that things are changing rapidly in Crosswordland.

"When I started more than ten years ago, if a word wasn't in one of three dictionaries it was out. Nowadays, because of electronic publishing, words get recognized far quicker – for example, 'iPod' and 'iPad' – well before getting into dictionaries. It's all subjective, but we must move with the times. I used to receive everything by snail mail, but now everything is so automated that I don't even have to deal with anyone else on the newspaper – which in a way makes things easier. I now lay out the page myself."

And Hugh is prepared to stick up for the puzzles. After a recent decision was made to shrink the size of the puzzle, Hugh called a meeting and kicked up such a storm that the management backed down and the crossword was restored to its normal size.

It was true that the issue provoking the most outrage from *Guardian* readers in the history of the newspaper was the decision to move the crossword from the back cover to the inside back cover. However, it is only recently that that record was broken. The subject matter could only have been, once again, the crossword. This time, the cryptic and quick puzzles were (foolishly) placed in the same section of the newspaper. Crossword-loving couples whose loyalties had been divided between the quick and the cryptic puzzles in the newspaper were no longer able to work on their favourite puzzles alone, without having to dismantle one section of the newspaper.

Hugh is evidently very fond of British cryptic crosswords. "In Britain we've taken the cryptic crossword further than in America and elsewhere.

"What's more, of course, the English language lends itself to wordplay a lot more than other languages. Linguistically, English is derived from so many sources, and we are likely to be able to create a greater variety of play on words ideas – far more say than French or Italian. And of course there are many words with different pronunciations and different meanings – 'lead' and 'lead' or 'polish' and 'Polish'."

As I say, I'm not entirely sure why the US hasn't taken to cryptic crosswords to the same extent.

"Perhaps it's because they don't have Kate Middleton," he adds, 'which I have just discovered is an anagram of 'naked tit model'."

Will Shortz

In the introduction to his *Favorite Sunday Crossword Puzzles*, Will Shortz, *New York Times* Crossword Editor and probably the most famous crosswording figure on the planet, asks whether crossword construction is an art or a craft.

His predecessor at the *NYT*, Eugene T. Maleska, had told Will he considered it "merely a craft".

And perhaps it was up to about the 1970s, when Shortz explains that "most American crosswords were merely collections of unrelated words, with the bulk of the answers and clues drawn from the dictionary."

Nowadays, however, Shortz adds, "Crossword construction has become at least a minor art."

"Constructions are sometimes breathtakingly daring," and "most of the regular *Times* puzzle contributors these days have distinctive voices."

Will is evidently very proud of his team. "Their humor, wit, ways with words, and areas of knowledge are all different. As a result they'll entertain and test you in different ways, too.

"To me this is the definition of art."

Born in 1952 on an Arabian horse farm in Crawfordsville, Indiana, Will Shortz is the world's only holder of a degree in Enigmatology, that from Indiana University. His thesis was written on pre-Civil War American word puzzles.

From a young age he proved an entrepreneur, selling his first puzzle to a youth magazine at the age of 14. At 16, he was finding work as a freelance puzzle writer.

Originally, Will had studied law at Virginia University, with the intention of making enough money in ten years to retire and simply write puzzles, his real dream. Ten years proved far too much, and immediately after graduating, he chose to head straight into the world of puzzledom.

Editor of the *New York Times* crossword since 1993, *Games Magazine* editor too, and founder and director of the American Crossword Puzzle Tournament, Will also owns the world's largest puzzle library, with tens of thousands of books, and magazines dating back to the sixteenth century.

The World Puzzle Championships is also his baby; the World Puzzle Federation too, founded in 1999.

He describes himself in the introduction to his *Favorite Crossword Puzzles* as "someone whose favorite movie of the year is rarely, if ever, named best picture" and as someone who "hardly ever does anything fashionable", which may explain why his work is followed by millions across the United States and beyond.

Syndicated to more than 300 other newspapers and journals, hundreds of book collections have been published, and the iconic puzzle is now available on mobiles, iOS devices, Kindle Fire, Nook and Blackberry.

It is under his editorship that constructor by-lines have been added to the puzzles. The policy of increasing difficulty as the week progresses is Will's too.

In his spare time Will is a very handy table tennis player, announcing on Twitter recently, "Played my 175th consecutive day of table tennis last night."

When Will sets out to do something, there are no half measures!

With kind permission from Will, here are his rules for submitting a *NYT* crossword, should you wish to have a go at constructing one.

1 The pattern of black-and-white squares must be symmetrical. Generally this rule means that if you turn the grid upside-down, the pattern will look the same as it does right side up.

2 Do not use too many black squares. In the old days of puzzles, black squares were not allowed to occupy more than 16 per cent of a grid. Nowadays there is no strict limit, in order to allow maximum flexibility for the placement of theme entries. Still, 'cheater' black squares (ones that do not affect the number of words in the puzzle, but are added to make constructing easier) should be kept to a minimum, and large clumps of black squares anywhere in a grid are strongly discouraged.

3 Do not use unkeyed letters (letters that appear in only one word across or down). In fairness to solvers, every letter has to appear in both an Across and a Down word.

4 Do not use two-letter words. The minimum word length is three letters.

5 The grid must have all-over interlock. In other words, the black squares may not cut the grid into separate pieces. A solver, theoretically, should be able to proceed from any section of the grid to any other without having to stop and start over.

6 Long theme entries must be symmetrically placed. If there is a major theme entry three rows down from the top of the grid, for instance, then there must be another theme entry in the same position three rows up from the bottom. Also, as a general rule, no non-theme entry should be longer than any theme entry.

7 Do not repeat words in the grid.

8 Do not make up words and phrases. Every answer must have a reference or else be in common use in everyday speech or writing.

The above rules apply to the crosswords in almost all publications. *The New York Times'* Crossword Specifications sheet lists some more special rules of the *Times*.

Further Specifications

The *New York Times* looks for intelligent, literate, entertaining and well-crafted crosswords that appeal to the broad range of *Times* solvers.

Themes should be fresh, interesting, narrowly defined and consistently applied throughout the puzzle. If the theme includes a particular kind of pun, for example, then all the puns should be of that kind. Themes and theme entries should be accessible to everyone (themeless daily puzzles using wide-open patterns are also welcome).

Constructors should emphasize lively words and names and fresh phrases. We especially encourage the use of phrases from everyday writing and speech, whether or not they are in the dictionary. For variety, try some of the lesser-used letters of the alphabet: J, Q, X, Z, K, W, etc. Brand names are acceptable if they're well-known nationally and you use them in moderation.

The clues in an ideal puzzle provide a well-balanced test of vocabulary and knowledge, ranging from classical subjects like literature, art, classical music, mythology, history, geography etc, to modern subjects like movies, TV, popular music, sports and names in the news. Clues should be accurate, colorful and imaginative. Puns and humor are welcome.

Do not use partial phrases longer than five letters (ONE TO A, A STITCH IN, for example), uninteresting obscurity (a Bulgarian village, a water bug genus, etc) or uncommon abbreviations or foreign words. Keep crosswordese to a minimum. Difficult words are fine – especially for the harder daily puzzles that get printed late in the week if the words are interesting bits of knowledge or useful additions to the vocabulary. However, never let two obscure words cross.

Maximum word counts: 78 words for a 15×15 (72 for an unthemed); 140 for a 21×21. Maximums may be exceeded slightly, at the editor's discretion, if the theme warrants.

Diagramless crosswords

Diagramless puzzles must be 17×17 in size. Follow the style as shown on the Sunday puzzle page. Puns 'n' Anagrams and Cryptics are done by assignment only.

Note: Times puzzles must never have been published anywhere before, either in print or electronically. *The Times* buys all rights, including first rights.

Format

Use regular typing paper (8½" 11"). Type the clues double-spaced on the left (no periods after the numbers), answer words in a corresponding column on the far right. Give a source for any hard to verify word or information. Down clues need not begin on a new page. Include a filled-in answer grid with numbers and a blank grid with numbers (for the editor's use). Put your name, address, and email address (if you have one) on the two grid pages. Only your name is needed on the other pages.

Send to:
Will Shortz, Crossword Editor
The New York Times
620 8th Ave.
New York, NY 10018

Please include an email address (preferred) or a stamped return envelope for reply.

Payment

$200 for a daily (15×15)
$1,000 for a Sunday puzzle (21×21)
$150 for a diagramless (17×17)
$200 for a novelty puzzle.

Note from the author: if you are simply happy remaining a solver, do please beware of the inevitable head-swelling side-effects, author Ambrose Bierce defining one particular word in his *The Devil's Dictionary* as follows:

Egotism (n.) Doing the *New York Times* crossword puzzle with a pen.

MIKE HUTCHINSON

Mike is the Crossword Editor at the *Independent* – and fellow Brightonian and football/soccer fan (albeit Tottenham Hotspur). I occasionally take Mike to see Brighton and Hove Albion play at our marvellous Amex stadium where I am a season ticket holder, in the North Stand (the stand for the most v,ociferous and foul-mouthed). Mike is a dab hand at the guitar, appearing in concert at our house-warming party, entertaining children of guests with a song about pirates. The kids loved it, but personally I had to switch my crossword brain off for the duration of the song as, on every iteration of the chorus, instead of the word 'pirates' I heard an anagram of 'traipse'.

Mike explains how his day goes:

"Nowadays crossword editors are expected to be familiar with computers and are involved with laying out the puzzles on the page to a greater or lesser extent. I receive puzzles from setters in various formats, but I need to produce a version of each in a program called InDesign that can be cut and pasted straight onto the newspaper page, as well as providing interactive versions for the *Independent* web site and lists of solutions for phone help/cheat lines.

"We editors, of course, have to deal with setters. There's a can of worms indeed. Diplomatically I'll say that most setters are a pleasure to deal with, but some can be a little precious about having their masterpieces tampered with. The way I see it, it's my job to get the best possible puzzles for our readers, and whether an improved clue is entirely the setter's own work or achieved with a bit of editorial interference is of little interest to most solvers.

"There are only two 'broadsheet' crossword editors who are also setters; me and Richard Browne at *The Times,* with whom I share a birthday.

"I think being a setter improves my editing and gives me more understanding of the setting process and therefore more empathy with the setters. A number of setters have suggested that it makes their lives a little easier that I understand the creative process.

"I was introduced to cryptic crosswords by my dad, a *Daily Mail* reader, but I didn't make much progress as a solver until I met a group of *Guardian* crossword aficionados at university. I set a few dreadful crosswords for my university student newspaper *The Beaver* (yes, really), but then one day, having left university, when I was working in a record shop, I saw an advert in the *Evening Standard* that began 'Do you like crosswords?' I did, and after going through a selection process which involved supplying cryptic clues for a list of words, got a job with Morley Adams Ltd, a Fleet Street agency which supplied a lot of the tabloids with their crosswords.

"Approximately 20 years later, I happened to be in the right place at the right time when the *Independent* needed a new crossword editor."

RICH NORRIS

I asked Rich, *LA Times* Crossword Editor, what he considers makes a great puzzle.

"For starters, originality. I love to see a puzzle idea I haven't seen before. That doesn't mean reinventing the wheel. A puzzle that introduces a new twist on an old theme is still original. For example, themes about birds have been done dozens of times, but constructor Elizabeth Long found a new approach by intersecting pairs of birds in the grid in T-shapes and calling the puzzle TBIRD.

"Greatness doesn't end with the theme. Contemporary, lively non-theme answers help to maintain the solver's interest level throughout the solving experience. I can best define 'lively' and 'interesting' with examples: MR CLEAN, MIND-SET, and LIKE NEW are lively. CLEANEST, MINDING, and LIKABLE— not so much.

"Last but not least, we like clues that are creative and fresh. That doesn't mean never repeating a clue that's been used before. Solvers often need that familiarity to get started. But it does mean thinking about each clue for more than a few seconds, trying to find an interesting and different approach that fits the puzzle's overall difficulty. Contrary to popular belief, easy clues don't have to be dull."

And how would Rich say the *LA Times* crossword differs from its peers, such as the *NYT*?

"Both puzzles progress in difficulty throughout the week, but our overall difficulty curve isn't as dramatic as at the NYT, which can get pretty hard as early as Thursday. For that reason, I think we're more accessible for new and less-experienced solvers, while at the same time we're challenging enough at the end of the week to keep skilled solvers entertained as well."

And Rich, for whom 2013 marks the 5000th puzzle under his editorship. is very proud of his constructing team.

"It's very hard to pick favorite constructors over the years, but with apologies to my loyal constructors past and present, I'd say that Dan Naddor was probably the most imaginative and prolific constructor I've ever known. He worked for me for about four years and unfortunately passed away in late 2009. Among his more outstanding puzzles are these two:

"A 'Battleship' puzzle, a rare asymmetrical grid with five randomly placed vessels (SUBMARINE, AIRCRAFT CARRIER, etc). The clues for the vessels all read [Part of the game]. The last vessel was BATTLESHIP, whose clue was [Part of the game, and the game itself]. Every other clue in the puzzle had either '(h)' or '(m)' after it, telling solvers whether it intersected a vessel (hit) or not (miss).

"A 'word chain' puzzle, with these six theme answers: STORE ROOM, SERVICE COURT, CASE HISTORY, CHANNEL SURF, BOARDING PASS, WORD CHAIN. The sequence forms a perpetual chain, since each phrase-ending word can pair with the beginning word of the next phrase (ROOM SERVICE, COURT CASE, etc). The beauty of the theme is not only in its symmetry, but also in the inclusion of WORD CHAIN as the final answer (CHAIN STORE makes the chain perpetual)."

Some neat and snappy clues from his puzzle team, perhaps simpler than UK word playing, but often pleasing nevertheless:

Doug Peterson:
1 Well-funded syndicates? (3-7)
2 Start of a rule broken by foreigners? (1,6,1)
3 Engaged in an undercover racket (6)

Bradley Wilber:
4 Bear aloft? (4)
5 His opening statement was famous (3,4)
6 Famous higher-up in admissions (2,5)
7 Hippie era swinger? (4,7)

Marti DuGuay-Carpenter:
8 State secrets? (4)
9 Mount Everest? (5)
10 Biblical mount? (3)
11 One making big bucks? (6)
12 Gave a bad impression? (6)

David Steinberg
13 Flashy company? (5)
14 It doesn't hold water (8)

And one from Rich:
15 Choose the window instead of the aisle? (5)

COLIN INMAN

Some questions answered, with the kind permission of Colin, who is Crossword
Editor at the *Financial Times*:

There are around 500–1,000 entries to the Saturday cryptic puzzle, and
around 200–500 for the Monday cryptic. *The Times* and the *Guardian* have
considerably more entries, perhaps 4,000.

Don't bother to use a large envelope. All entries are assembled as in a filing
cabinet. An envelope is chosen, and then a random number is counted either to
that envelope's right, or to its left.

The number of entries seems to be unaffected by the difficulty of the puzzle.
Fewer entries are received, however, after a fine summer weekend (if, indeed,
there are any such weekends in any given British summer!).

The number of female winners seems to be disproportionate to what would be
expected of the *FT*'s readership.

Colin describes the average *FT* crossword solver as "someone on a crowded
train on the way to or from the office. My aim is therefore is to ensure the
puzzle should ideally be solvable in a reasonable time and without the use of
dictionaries or electronic aids."

Here is a little about the team of *FT* setters. It's pretty representative of
the types of people you find on all crossword teams on many other British
newspapers. Many of these names also set crosswords for other British
newspapers, and for papers on other shores.

Dante, Roger Squires, is the longest-serving of present *FT* compilers. He was
listed for many years in the *Guinness Book of Records* as the world's most
prolific compiler.

Highlander, David Shenton, is a retired oil industry executive who lives in
northern Scotland, hence his pseudonym.

Cinephile, Rev. John Graham, appearing as Araucaria in the *Guardian* has been
setting puzzles for the *FT* since 1983. Origin of the pseudonyms: an araucaria is
a monkey-puzzle tree while Cinephile is an anagram of Chile pine, a similar tree.
Cinephile is now in his 93rd year, his wit and originality are undimmed.

Dogberry, John Young, the pseudonym being taken from the incoherent
constable in *Much Ado About Nothing*, who 'is too cunning to be understood'.
Young has worked as a transcriber and encoder on various historical works,
including John Foxe's *Book of Martyrs*; his present job is as Transcription and
Tagging Manager for the Newton Project at Sussex University, which aims to
put all of Isaac Newton's works online. This is, perhaps, the most unusual day
job among our compilers.

Adamant, Hazel Goldman, née Damant, is one of only two female compilers. She appears elsewhere as Evesham.

Cincinnus, Michael Curl, has a crossword website at www.bestforpuzzles.com. The site includes a selection of his old *FT* and *Guardian* crosswords (as Orlando), and helpful features for crossword solvers, including a cryptic crossword tutorial and dictionary. 'Cincinnus' is a Latin word meaning 'curl'. This is the derivation of the cognomen of the Roman hero Cincinnatus (literally 'curly-haired') who was a paragon of honesty and simplicity!

Armonie, John Dawson, formerly a chemical engineer, lives in semi-retirement in Kendal. He too hosts a website at www.lakedistrictwalks.com; nothing to do with crosswords but describing dozens of walks in that beautiful part of the world.

Mudd, John Halpern, aka Paul (the *Guardian*), Dada (the *Daily Telegraph*), Punk (the *Independent*), Anon (*The Times*)

Phssthpok, Adam Sanitt, is a lawyer working in London. His first *FT* crossword appeared in 1994, when he was 21. Phssthpok is a character in Larry Niven's book *Protector*.

Orense, Jeremy Mutch, for many years a contracts manager in the tourism industry, learnt about setting crosswords from his friend Bert Danher. Orense is the name of the town in Spain where he spent a year as part of his degree course.

Gozo, Tom Johnson, is a retired teacher. He is a UK bus enthusiast, but "Maltese and Gozo buses were just that little bit special until 2011, when Arriva took over!", he says. He edits and compiles as Doc for the *Spectator* crossword and edits Araucaria's *1 Across* magazine as well as setting Polymath general knowledge crosswords for the *FT* and for *Prospect* magazine, where he appears as Didymus.

Crux, Colin Garside, is another retired teacher, also influenced by Bert Danher. Crux in *Chambers Dictionary* is 'Something that creates difficulty or perplexity, a puzzle'.

Moodim, Alex Jagger, originally had two cats called Moo and Dim. They are now dead but the pseudonym remains. She lives and works in Cumbria.

Bradman, Don Manley, also appears in other papers as various Dons: Pasquale, Duck, Quixote, Giovanni. He edits the *Church Times* crossword and is the author of *Chambers Crossword Manual*, now in its fourth edition. He worked for more than 30 years in academic and educational publishing, but since 2002 has been a full-time compiler/editor.

Neo, Paul Bringloe, is a freelance advertising copywriter. He is also the drummer for several bands, including prog-rockers Blind Panic, with whom he has just finished recording an album. Neo is the lead character in *The Matrix,* a movie that posits – like crossword clues? – every kind of reality and unreality as alternatives to what's actually there.

Falcon, Allan Scott, has set the Everyman crossword in the *Observer* since 1994 and also sets puzzles for *The Times* and the *Daily Telegraph*. Robert Falcon Scott was the name of the explorer.

Sleuth, Philip Marlow, works as a freelance TV producer specializing in documentaries and drama documentaries about politics, current affairs and history. Elsewhere he appears as Hypnos and Shamus. His pseudonym is homage to his near namesake, the fictional detective Philip Marlowe.

Monk, Mark Kelmanson, is Professor of Applied Mathematics at the University of Leeds during the daytime and (voluntary) dry-stone waller in West Yorkshire whenever possible. The pseudonym derives from M on K.

Io, John Henderson, has a crossword website at www.enigmatist.co.uk, the name under which he compiles crosswords for the *Guardian*.
    Note from the author: Prior to my continuing 'dry' years, John and I were drinking pals for some years around the dens of north London. John was also amazing when he instigated and participated in the creation of several puzzles themed around my marriage to Taline. Five puzzles were published in many of the national newspapers on our wedding day, July 31, 2011, to our utter delight.

Jason, Paul McKenna, spends his time between building oil and gas pipelines and the study of Hellenistic poetry of the third to second century BC. The pseudonym is young-sounding, heroic (the *Argonautica* of Apollonius Rhodius), and duplicitous (the lead male character in Euripides' *Medea*).

Flimsy, Anthony Plumb, is a primary school teacher working in Lincolnshire. He also produces thematic puzzles for the *Independent* magazine.

Aardvark, Mike Warburton, embarked on a freelance writing career after the closure of a family sports business. Now he specializes in setting crosswords for the *Independent* and the *Daily Telegraph* as well as the *FT*. He admits to having chosen Aardvark as his pseudonym because he has a long nose!

Alberich, Neil Shepherd, lives in the Czech Republic and is an ardent Wagnerite, hence the pseudonym.

SECTION 4
CROSSWORD STORIES, FANS AND CELEBRITY FANS

CHAPTER 11
CROSSWORD STORIES, FURTHER THOUGHTS AND COMMENT FROM AROUND THE WORLD

THE BENEFITS OF CROSSWORD SOLVING

Although more and more younger solvers are taking up the challenge of a daily cruciverbal fix, there is a preconception that the 'average' solver is in their sixties or beyond. While there are always going to be a handful of nonagenarians who sky-dive on the days they are in recovery from night-clubbing, most are seeking more cerebral pursuits to keep that grey matter active and alert.

Neuropsychologist Kaz Pasiecznik, a former researcher in the Memory Group at Bristol University's Psychology Department, says that his studies and research into how the brain and mind work, with particular focus on memory, gave him a deeper fascination with cryptic crosswords and the application and development of vocabulary networks, memory access and analytic thinking.

You can also sign up to one of his courses on how to solve cryptic crosswords at www.crosswordtutors.co.uk.

"Crossword solving has so many benefits that it's not surprising they are so popular," says Kaz.

Here he lists and explains some of them:

Increasing the vocabulary: "The obvious tangible benefit is an improved passive vocabulary, i.e. words which you understand the meaning of when you read or hear them. What people don't always appreciate is the improvement to active vocabulary – that is, words that you use yourself when writing or speaking. The knock-on effect of this is that my students find they are better writers, be it letters, poetry, song lyrics, reports, or just texts and emails!"

Fluency: "Linked to the above point, I believe crossword solving strengthens the network of brain cells which represent your vocabulary, making it easier to get words out – so with a combination of a bigger active vocabulary – more words at your mental finger tips – and faster thinking speed, people find regular crossword solving makes them better verbal communicators, be it impressing in work meetings, entertaining friends, or public speaking."

Problem solving: "To solve a challenging crossword requires analytic ability, thinking outside the box, strategizing, trial-and-error, not to mention motivation, patience and perseverance! The list of auxiliary benefits of crossword solving is extensive, and still widely underestimated."

Social benefits: "It's time we got rid of the stereotype that crossword solving is only a solo activity – not only are several heads better than one, but solving with friends and family is great fun! The first thing I tell my course students to do is to say their thoughts out loud, and I encourage people to continue this habit after they leave the classroom. This is because there are several routes into your memory of words, including one via your auditory system, and one via your visual system. Thus by saying your thoughts aloud you give your brain another chance to hit upon the right answer. A similar argument runs for working with others – all our brains are wired up differently, and even though *you* hearing a word might not trigger your brain to think of the answer, your friend hearing you say a word might trigger their brain to think of the right answer."

Aiding the memory: "It is widely believed, and indeed promoted by many medical professionals, that regular crossword solving makes for a healthier brain and slows the ageing process, i.e. making your memory last longer."

(It is arguably this last point, about slowing the ageing process, that is proving the most powerful. Of course, it is in one's twilight years that the menace of a particularly prevalent and debilitating disease can take hold.)

CROSSWORDS IN THE FIGHT AGAINST ALZHEIMER'S.

In the early 1990s, top US puzzle constructor Merl Reagle and his wife Marie had been planning a move to Oregon when Marie's father suddenly died, and Marie found herself the primary caregiver for her mother Jo, who had just been diagnosed with Alzheimer's disease.

The Reagles' Oregon move was put on hold, and they moved to Florida to care for Jo through her last few, desperately tough, years.

Seeing the painful impact of Alzheimer's on its sufferers and those close to them, Merl wanted to use his fame in the crossword business to give something back. He set up the National Brain Game Challenge, an online Sunday puzzle with a hidden secret message that is the key to solving the contest. The entry fee is $25, and the first prize in each of the two separate player categories of 'Casual solver' and 'Puzzle professionals' is $2,500. All proceeds go to the Alzheimer's Foundation of America (AFA), via www.alxfdn.org

This from the AFA website:

"Research suggests that regular mental workouts may help reduce the risk of Alzheimer's disease—an incurable brain disorder that is increasing in incidence nationwide and primarily affects the older population. Flexing and stretching your brain, just like flexing and stretching other parts of your body, is critical for a successful ageing workout—so much so that experts suggest that people of all ages exercise both their brains and bodies on a daily basis. Research suggests that regular mental activities might help reduce the risk of Alzheimer's disease or other memory disorders by:

Enhancing cognitive reserve

Stimulating growth of new brain cells, and

Maintaining or strengthening connections between brain cells."

Merl adds:

"I keep hearing about studies that show a direct connection between brain exercise, such as solving hard crosswords, and a delay in the onset of the disease.

"The oft-cited reason is that such brain-exercising activities help grow dendrites, and the more dendrites one has going into old age, the better one's chances are of keeping Alzheimer's at bay. Almost on a weekly basis I hear from older solvers who feel that their puzzle solving is keeping the disease away, and I say, more power to them. Percentage-wise, crossword solvers seem to get Alzheimer's a lot less than people who don't engage in some form of brain exercise. Personally, I do wonder about certain things – such as, if a puzzle fan doesn't get Alzheimer's, is it because of the actual crossword-solving process or because the person's brain was genetically predisposed in that direction, which is why they naturally took up crosswords in the first place?

"What keeps me hopeful about the whole crosswords/Alzheimer's issue is the dendrites angle – the more you have, the better off your brain is. As I once heard a doctor say, a person may die of heart disease at 85 because their crossword solving had pushed back the onset of their Alzheimer's until age 90."

(Since founding the National Brain Game challenge in 2011, the cause has become even more personal: Merl's own mother has been diagnosed with the disease.)

THE COMPLETION PROCESS – FIGURE THIS OUT!

Most solvers would surely just pick up a puzzle, solve some or all of it, and then move on. But that evidently is not enough for some of us – for example, a certain Dr S. Naranan.

Naranan, an experimental cosmic ray physicist and X-ray astronomer (worth an exclamation mark in parentheses (!)) began wondering if there was a pattern to how frequently we are able to complete the whole grid, and to the number of clues left unsolved.

Based on a staggering ten years collecting data from his solving attempts, he concluded that the occurrence of failures follows the Negative Binomial Distribution. This is the same distribution used by the car insurance industry to predict the probability of accidents, or by marketing teams to forecast purchase patterns for a product.

Dr Naranan's research paper has been published in the *Journal of Quantitative Linguistics*, and details here are courtesy of www.crosswordsunclued.com.

Naranan states, 'The Negative Binomial Distribution (NBD) depends on two parameters (p, k), the parameters that quantify the gap between the setter and solver. These parameters are related to the average and standard deviation of the distribution of failures.

In mathematical terms, if the average is m and the standard deviation is s, then p is $(m/s*s)$, the ratio of average to variance and $k = mp/(1-p)$. Another way to look at p and k: The number of puzzles with no errors is $p^{\wedge}k$. The ratio of puzzles with errors $x = 1$ and $x = 0$ is $k (1-p)$.

This means if a solver tells how many of his puzzles have $x = 0$ (no errors) and how many have $x = 1$ (one error) from a known sample of puzzles, this model can predict the entire distribution, i.e. how many will have 2, 3, 4, etc. number of errors.

But what about solvers with differing skill levels? NBD can effectively model the (p, k) for solvers with different solving expertise.

According to the model described, the complexity of crossword puzzles and their variability will depend both on the solver and the composer(s). There is no reason to suppose the NBD will not apply universally to all crossword puzzles and solvers. So, for each solver of crossword puzzles, one can expect NBD to apply, each with a characteristic pair of parameters (p, k) that quantifies the gap between the skills of the composer and solver. For the author $(p, k) = (0.455, 0.869)$.

The perfect solver, who never makes an error in the puzzle, has $x = 0$ always. So Prob $(x = 0) = 1$ and Prob $(x) = 0$ for all other x. For such a solver, $p = 1$ and $k = $ anything.

So there you have it. And for those of you with a fear of Negative Binomial Distribution, you can now come out from behind the sofa.

SOME XIMENEAN VS LIBERTARIAN RESEARCH

In 1997, further research was being undertaken by a crossword fanatic from Sunderland, England.

As part of his MSc in Social Research Methods and Statistics at City University, London, David Moore, these days Managing Editor at a puzzle magazine publishers, wrote a dissertation on the Ximenean versus the non-Ximenean cryptic clues appearing in two British national newspapers.

"It was marked with distinction," he says, "so it can't all have been nonsense.

"I took somewhere near 500 randomly selected clues from the previous 20 years of each of the *Independent* and the *Guardian*, categorized them not just into the standard types of clue (usually identified as being eight to twelve clue types), but also into all the different smaller elements I could identify. I think it came to about 30 (including the use of Roman numerals, abbreviations, first and last letters, etc as individual techniques).

"I also counted all the instances of techniques that had become so standard as to be part of the language of crosswords, instantly gettable without any requirement for creative thought. This gave some pretty clear stats on who seemed to expend the least energy in clue creating. I can't mention any names.

"I also gave them separate classifications as Ximenean or Libertarian (I might have called it Araucarian). Most difficult were those penny-dropping cryptic definition ones, which I generally wasn't able to categorize any further in the time and resources I had, but they certainly weren't all the same at all.

"Classifying them as non-Ximenean was difficult in some cases, as it was often via simply using a superfluous word, whereas at other times, particularly with a lot of Araucaria's clues, qualifying the technique he *had* actually used was more than my poor brain could pin down – I just got it, but wasn't always sure why it made sense.

"In the end I was surprised to discover that crosswords across the samples from both newspapers had roughly the same proportion of not-strictly Ximenean clues – about one in 20.

"But I'm not convinced the nature of the variance was the same. Sometimes it was simply a case of what I judged to be use of a superfluous word, which I might later have classified as a valid context-setting connector.

"I'm also fairly certain that, rightly or wrongly, I found one clue by Don Manley that I classified as being non-Ximenean. I made a point of mentioning this in my final write-up!

"My overall impression was that the standard of difficulty and the consistency of style varied far more across the *Guardian* than the *Independent*, but overall I didn't want to say that I thought either paper was easier than the other. The *Guardian* reached far higher levels of fun and creativity overall, but it plumbed far lower depths of banal turgidity as well.

"While the *Independent* stuck pretty rigidly in those days to a particular reliable style, the *Guardian* was much more of a something-for-everyone lucky dip, the senators seated across the house from a rogues' gallery, separated by a group of wishy-washy liberals."

SOME TONGUE-TWISTING?

Richard Rogan runs marathons in under three hours, and sets some of the more challenging cryptic crosswords for *The Times*. Though now working as an IT consultant and specialist, he spent many years employed as a linguist.

Here Richard discusses how the puzzle might fare in other languages.

"As a crossword setter who speaks French reasonably fluently and has a fair knowledge of Russian, I've sometimes thought about how cryptic crosswords would work in those – and indeed other – languages. I've always assumed the received wisdom to be that English is not merely the optimum language for the cryptic clue but the only one. Is that fair?

"There are plenty of appealing possibilities, answer-wise, in French while Russian, being a language where so many words are built from smaller ones, would seem also to offer lots of promise. And I defy a Russian crossword compiler worth his or her salt *not* to exploit the delightful coincidence that the words for 'already' and 'narrower' are spelt the same, albeit with the stress on different syllables.

"The problem is in the actual cluing, of course: English is ideal for the sort of clue we are used to seeing in *The Times* Crossword, for example, where one can clue 'UFO' as: 'Object to puzzle going over one's head'. Surface-wise we are led to think of an unfairly obscure crossword, whereas of course the actual meaning is very different: 'object' is really a noun and 'puzzle' a verb, while 'over one's head' is to be taken literally.

"In short, there's a 'flexibility' (some would call it looseness) about English that is largely syntax-based, allowing juxtaposition of words and phrases such that their meaning can be read in more than one way. And, of course, the above clue is also a reminder of how often, as native English speakers, we are often more inclined to take the metaphorical meaning of a phrase rather than the literal! There's no reason, though, why cryptic clues can't work in other languages; they'd just be different, to suit the medium in which they are written. We shouldn't expect otherwise, or indeed be disappointed by the fact."

WHY ALL THE TESTOSTERONE?

We have spoken with a lot of blokes in this book. But my experience is that the solving community is pretty evenly balanced, around 50 per cent men, 50 per cent women.

Sarah Hayes, aka Arachne, discusses why the crossword construction industry appears to be so male-dominated.

"At crossword social events people do occasionally notice that I'm a woman and are sometimes kind enough to point it out to me, but essentially I'm a setter who happens to be female, rather than a female setter, if you see what I mean. The real question is surely not so much 'Why so many male setters?' as 'Why so few female?' and to this it's hard to find a plausible answer. Women are at least as 'good with words' as men, and we solve crosswords in droves, so why do so few of us take the next step, into setting? Answers on a postcard, please, because I really haven't the foggiest. It's undoubtedly the case that the world of crossword setting is dominated by men, but if any women out there are being put off by a mental image of these chaps as a herd of rutting wildebeest, then let me say that in my experience they're much more like a basket of kittens. Let's get one thing absolutely clear about the world of setting, in words of one syllable: *There. Is. No. Sex. Ism.* So come on in, sisters, the water's lovely.

"The world of solving is, alas, another matter. Until fairly recently it had never occurred to me that gender might be an issue in Crosswordland, but a perfectly ordinary and innocuous clue of mine caused such a palaver that a radical rethink was needed:

"Woman in charge of automobile club (6)

"A simple double definition of DRIVER, which can mean either 'someone in charge of an automobile' or 'a kind of golf club'. Case closed? Not on your Nelly. *Guardian* readers (***Guardian*** readers!*) in some numbers were bamboozled, perplexed or dismayed by the simple notion that a motorist might in fact be a woman. Mental feats of Byzantine complexity were performed to try to explain the presence of this presumptuous female at the wheel of a car (was it instead something to do with either of the actresses Minnie or Betty Driver, perhaps?) but in the end a dispiriting number of solvers remained convinced the clue was unfair. That was the day I girded my feminist loins for a long insurgency, and unfortunately the sexists still take the bait every time. My work here is not yet done."

*For those readers from outside of the little island of Britain, the stereotypical *Guardian* reader is often perceived as being a middle-class, eco-warrior liberal.

BEDROOM ANTICS

At a recent talk I gave about the lives of cryptic crossword setters, a gentleman in his later years approached me to offer a mild ticking-off for my having described 'Nam' as 'War' in a recent puzzle. He was probably right to do so. Fair do's.

But this gentleman had something else to share. He wished to thank me.

Ushering me away from prying ears, he shared that, for him and his wife, "your crosswords have replaced our sex life."

"Though not immediately obvious to the discerning reader, there are a number of distinct similarities between those arcane arts of cruciverbalism and of fornication.

"There's something pleasurable to fill in. While doing it, phone calls from the mother-in-law are most unwelcome.

"And of course, a rubber is firmly recommended."

Which brings me to a personal favourite clue, I believe penned by the late Mike Laws, former *Times* crossword editor, and great setter in his own right.

Mad, passionate lovers (7)

The gentleman I met that day (and his wife) were certainly mad – in the keen sense. And they also were passionate – if not, these days, 'BONKERS'.

SOME CROSSWORD 'JOKES'

Much like a cryptic crossword clue, a good joke often works on wordplay. Ask a friend to rearrange the Scrabble letters S, N, I, P, E to form a body part. Very few will come up with SPINE.

Here's a good 'un:

'What's pink and hard in the mornings? (3,9,5,9)'

It is an old joke of course, describing the puzzle in the famous pastel-shaded London-based daily, 'The *Financial Times* Crossword'. I asked Colin Inman, the *FT* crossword editor to see if he could recall this clue that I swear I witnessed some years ago. He couldn't. Have I imagined it maybe?

Here's another:

How many crossword solvers does it take to change a light bulb? (3)

And here's a personal favourite:

'The busiest postman in the world'

If you are asking yourself 'how many letters?' you have unwittingly become the stooge.

The answer is of course: MILLIONS.

A COSTLY MISTAKE

Then there was the notorious 1997 attempt by the *Telegraph* crossword editor Val Gilbert to substitute the current cryptic crossword team with recycled puzzles from the previous few years. According to Roger Squires, most of the compilers were prepared to accept their fate, but he and Ruth Crisp, a long-standing and much respected setter in her own right, decided they were going to fight it, and fight they did.

Roger Squires takes up the story, as recounted on Derek Harrison's Crossword Centre website www.crossword.org.uk:

"In May 1997 Val Gilbert, the *Telegraph* crossword editor, informed setters that she was undertaking an experiment in July and no crosswords would be required for that period. July's puzzles turned out to be an odd mixture of styles and we all recognized some of our old clues.

"Michael Mepham had worked with Val in the past, providing a computer program that immediately converted the compilers' clues and grids into the published form. We understood he had had a database of *Telegraph* and *Mail* clues for the previous 14 years.

"In November Val wrote to us telling us to expect 'seismic changes' with the clincher coming on February 5, 1998, when we were informed that technology had caught up with us and no crosswords were required after March 30. However, she would pay £2 per clue, exclusive for the *Telegraph*, were it good enough to be included in her database of over 42,000 clues.

"Some setters accepted their fate, but Ruth Crisp and I joined forces to fight this decision. We felt the more people that knew about it the better. I managed to spread the news of this action in the media thanks to help from Brian Greer and Mike Laws in *The Times* – Mike also mentioned it on the radio – Francis Wheen at *Private Eye* (three times), known crossword fans, the *Guardian* Diary, The Crossword Club, my local *Shropshire Star*, etc.

"Eventually Val felt she had to respond to this and she combined with Tom Uttley to write a 'news' article on March 20, 1998 defending her position.

"Reaction from readers was not good.

"On the morning of April 1 I received a call from the then deputy editor of the *Telegraph*, later London Mayor, Boris Johnson, asking for my views of the situation, which I gave somewhat forcibly. I suggested he then ring Ruth who also vigorously gave her opinions. Later that day, Boris rang again 'to eat humble pie' and to inform us that we would all be reinstated. An article by him, reiterating this, appeared on April 2, 1998.

"Following this we were invited to our first lunch at Canary Wharf and we received an immediate rise in the crossword fee."

Roger adds an interesting postscript:

"When the sackings were mooted, I was contacted by Robin Esser, a director of the *Daily Mail*, suggesting we meet for lunch at The Garrick in London to hear an idea he had. I went and he suggested I keep selected *Telegraph* setters together and act as a crossword editor for the *Mail* cryptics, which he thought weren't good enough. We had other meetings (I was paid expenses and he claimed for working lunches!) and it was all set to go, with four other setters, when Val capitulated."

ABANDONING SHIPS
In 1982, asked to put aside his favourite crossword puzzle before the end of his tea break, a shop steward at the Scott Lithgow shipyard on Glasgow's River Clyde refused to until work resumed. All workers downed tools, and a major two-week strike ensued.

THE SLOWEST SOLVE?
For many years the *Guinness Book of Records* described a woman who had taken 34 years to complete *The Times* crossword. What actually happened, according to a letter found in *The Times* archive, was that a woman had been clearing out her loft when she came across an old *Times* newspaper, part of the wrapping for a carpet, with the puzzle unfinished. She decided to finish it, which she did. Someone wrote to *The Times* to tell the paper that they might be interested in knowing this had happened, but it was soon being told that she had been trying for thirty-four years to do so, and had finally been successful.

A LITTLE FUN ...
The world's smallest crossword puzzle was created by the giant of British comedy Spike Milligan, whose poem *Rain* we shall meet later. Called the 'Crossword for Idiots', the clues to the one-square teaser were as follows:

Across
1 The indefinite article
Down
1 First letter of alphabet

... AND A LOT OF FUN

A crossword grid 30 m (100 feet) high forms an entire external wall of a
residential building in the city of Lvov in the Ukraine. Clues to the 34 × 19
puzzle can be found across the city. As night falls, fluorescent letters placed
inside squares on the building become visible and so the solution is revealed.

CLIP ART

So that's a big crossword. But arguably the world's biggest crossword fan is Raju
Umamaheshwar. He collects clippings on his favourite puzzles, and over the
years has accumulated quite a few. Let me quantify 'quite a few' – Raju has, to
date, 400,000 clippings! Raju has a lot of explaining to do:

"I used to get my cuttings from the newspapers at the Nairobi Club Library,
thanks to a kind girl at the desk who used to do them for me, so painstakingly,
each week when the papers were taken off the reading desks. All crosswords
from *The Times*, the *Daily Telegraph*, the *Guardian*, the *Independent*, the
Spectator etc. were collected, and these formed the major part of the numbers.
Here, in Coimbatore, I get them from the Club at my residence, where they
get cut out of the *Hindu*, *Economic Times* and, the *Financial Standard* from an
obliging villa neighbour.

"Besides, anywhere any time, if I can get hold of some unusual ones, these
are also taken. At home, I buy the *New Indian Express*, the *Times of India* and
the *Deccan Chronicle*. My sister-in-law in Bombay sends me the clippings of
whatever she can lay her hands on. Hence, my daily harvest keeps piling. I bless
all these kind souls for assisting in my passion.

"I have been solving crosswords since my college days in Bombay, and used to
throw them away once done. However, whilst I was in Kenya I came across the
Limca Book of Records in which I found entries for such obscure things as the
largest collection of key chains, etc having been recorded. So I thought, why not
my crosswords which I hold so dear?

"This was in late 1990 and then I started collecting both unsolved and solved
crosswords, and just for a lark I sent the details of the first lot to the people at
Limca. *The Limca Book of Records* is mainly for records created by Indians
anywhere in the world. Thereafter I have been updating my tally each year and
have continuously been featured in the book, without a break."

In 2008, Raju organized an exhibition of his clippings in Nairobi, which
he says was well attended and was given extensive radio and TV coverage,
"particularly as it was [perhaps unsurprisingly!] the only crossword clippings
exhibition in Kenya."

And of course, this particular puzzle fan does like to solve the odd puzzle
– or two:

"I do a daily minimum of 20 puzzles, but on one occasion that did rise to
85. Crossword solving dominates all of my leisure time, while travelling by
car, train and by air. I haven't taken the wheel of my car here in Coimbatore,

thanks to my obliging wife who drives around with me doing the crosswords, next to her, hearing all her curses against the traffic hazards on the road. And whilst on holiday, I do as many as I can, to knock up the numbers. My cuttings and published books are meticulously packed in the luggage. I note down the place, time, date and day I solved each in a diary."

CROSSWORD BLOOPERS

In a crossword-setting career, we hopefully make only a few errors, but when we do let slip a slip, we certainly get to hear about it!

Geographical errors are the worst. In a *Guardian* puzzle a few years back, rather than North Yorkshire, I placed the town of Settle in the county of Cumbria. Cue meltdown at the *Guardian* switchboard. It seems everyone in the north of England just had to let the newspaper know of my incompetence.

They were right to do so. We must be kept on our toes and, as a small token of (almost) unreserved apology, I wrote a puzzle in which I certainly had to 'Settle up' at 1 across, but that at the next solution perhaps those who rang in about the error should now 'Settle down'. On another occasion I placed the Atacama Desert (at least partially) in Peru, rather than Chile. I had been constructing a Peruvian based theme in preparation for my charity trek to Machu Picchu, and had wanted to get as much 'Peru' in the puzzle as possible. A _ A _ A _ A fitted, and squinting at a map of South America from a distance, that particular desert seemed to lie along the border of Peru – at a push. What on earth had I been thinking, and how dare I assume I could get away with it? Any lapse in crossword integrity and the solver will find you out every time, without fail.

From the days when crossword grids were filled with pencil or ink, one particular crossword writer resolved always to double-check his puzzles after one slight error. After all, at a squint the letters 'D' and 'P' do look pretty similar.

A puzzle of his had gone to press in an Irish newspaper (of all places!) with the clue: 'Idiot, ass (4)'. Of course, he had intended the solution to be DOPE.

BLASTED CROSSWORDS

Irish setter Brian Greer had the task of sending the Azed Victor Verborum cup for winning his clue-writing competition to a Rear-Admiral Ridley who, on receiving an unexpected parcel from Belfast, scooped up the suspicious package, hurried it into the garden and dunked it into a bucket of water.

ONE ACROSS, SIX FEET DOWN

Our record-breaking crossword friend Roger Squires has provided over the years a number of personal crosswords for weddings and anniversaries, etc.

A puzzle had been requested on the death of a solver's mother, who had apparently solved Squires' crossword every week in the local *Telford Journal* for some years. Roger produced a grid in which the central black squares produced a large cross, surrounded by all the words that meant so much during this lady's life. The crossword was photographed, attached to a large wreath and lowered into the grave with her.

On another occasion former *Telegraph* crossword editor Val Gilbert sent Roger a cutting from the paper showing one of his puzzles partially completed. The puzzle had been found alongside the body of a woman who, evidently in a hurry, had scribbled her final wishes upon the crossword. The bereaved family asked lawyers to ascertain whether or not this was a legal will.

Ensuing court proceedings declared it valid.

SOLVING CRIME

One type of puzzle popular in tabloid Britain through the 1950s and into the 1970s was sometimes called 'The Jackpot' or 'Whichword'. Roger Squires takes up the story:

"A simple 13×13 grid was used with about 22 solutions required. Each of these needed the solver to add a missing word. We compilers were paid to make every one of these words have at least one alternative choice. *The Syndicate*, a crossword supplier run by Nigel Gee, chief crossword editor of *Central Press Features*, was asked to provide some puzzles for South African newspapers. The puzzles were sent, and each paper's editor would arbitrarily choose each answer.

"However, in 1974, Gee received a letter from a man purporting to be the chairman of the Kumalo School Parent Teachers Association, based in Bulawayo. The correspondent said he had received copies of two of these 'Whichword' crosswords, and would like to use them for fundraising, but urgently required the answers, which 'had been mislaid'. The letter was signed by an L. Simpson.

"Nigel knew these puzzles had been bought by the Durban paper, the *Sunday Tribune*, and had been published but not closed, so contacted them.

"The *Tribune* told Gee that a Henri Roussot often entered this competition and, on holiday from Rhodesia, had recently handed over 2,048 permutated entries' and paid 512 Rand. All were wrong. Roussot had then asked for the supplier's address as he 'wanted to see how the puzzles were put together'.

"We worked out that, if the editor were deciding the solutions, with twenty-two variables, it would be possible to have many thousands of wrong entries. At this time the prize had not been won and prize money was 20,000 Rand – and rising every week. This could carry on, taking the punters' money, until the editor arbitrarily selected the answers to find a single winner.

"The paper called in the police, they informed the local Bulawayo constabulary, and Mr Roussot, a survey technician in the Rhodesian Surveyor-General's Office, was interviewed. The paper reported the situation, but he denied it, even the fact that the PTA box number had been changed to his number. But eventually he capitulated and admitted it."

The Jackpot crossword ran for many years, and was very popular in the UK.

However, UK law now insists that a valid reason for every solution must be provided.

MORE CROSSWORD DEATHS AND TRAGEDIES

In March 1926, a man walked into Café Emke in Budapest, downed a coffee, and then attempted to make a call on the café's telephone, but apparently without success.

According to the Hungarian newspaper *Az Est*, minutes later a cloakroom attendant heard two bangs coming from the toilet, where a young man was found pistol in hand, blood gushing from his head and chest.

The man, who had apparently been living in misery and unemployment for some time, was identified as Antal Gyula. In his pocket a suicide note was found in the form of a crossword, *Az Est* adding that "the complexity of the crossword means that it has not yet been deciphered."

In 1994, tragedy befell a car and passenger ferry, the *MS Estonia*, going down in the Baltic Sea with the loss of 950 lives. An alert reader of the *Telegraph* noted that he had just solved a puzzle of Roger's which included the entries HMS HOOD (a battle cruiser that had gone down with the loss of 1400 lives), MASTER MARINER and ESTONIA. The puzzle had appeared in the newspaper a mere four days before the disaster.

Roger adds: "I do remember that the word in that slot was actually going to be ERITREA, but I changed it at the last minute, though I'm not sure why."

In 1990, a day after the assassination by the IRA of Conservative MP Ian Gow, a clue in the *Telegraph* crossword read 'Outcry caused by Tory assassination (4,6).'

Answer: BLUE MURDER'. After the first edition a sub-editor quickly substituted the clue for another. The offending clue had been written some weeks earlier.

FURTHER CRUCIVERBAL CRIME

In Melbourne in 1947, a 17-year old girl asking directions to a relative's home was assaulted by a 25-year old salesman, after luring her to his own address instead. Going to the police, the girl reeled off the answers to a half-completed crossword she had seen on the premises and memorized. The man was subsequently arrested and charged.

AN INSIDE JOB – TONY FONTAINE, AKA 'FIDELIO'

The inventive and often puzzling Tony Fontaine set cryptic crosswords for the *Guardian* from his cell in Maidstone Prison. In one of his puzzles the compulsive fraudster wrote a clue for his own pseudonym, FIDELIO (the name of Beethoven's only opera, whose plot describes the rescue of a prisoner), as an anagram of 'Oi I fled', a clue presumably written during one of his brief periods of liberation.

LIVE AMMUNITION – AND BLANKS

You know that feeling when you're dying to know the answer to something? In 1925, a Mr Koerner of Brooklyn, an adjuster for the New York Telephone Company, had just that feeling.

Asking his wife for a little assistance in completing his crossword, she declared she was too tired and headed off to bed. The thought of being left alone with his torment evidently proved too much to bear. A few minutes later the bedroom door opened and Mrs Koerner was confronted by her husband wielding a pistol. A scream, a flash and a burning sensation on her temple later, she fled from the house, pursued by her husband, firing for a second time.

Safely around the corner, there was a third shot. The crossword had evidently proved too much, and her husband lay dead in the street, a bullet in his heart.

AN UNFORTUNATE COINCIDENCE?

I have trained my mother to call, and pamper my ego after the publication of every puzzle of mine, which to her credit she does unfailingly. She solves the *Guardian* puzzles and then tells me what she thinks of them, but also lets me know where she considers I could do with pulling up my cruciverbal socks. And sometimes there are queries. A few years back after one particular puzzle, true to form, my mother rang.

"Good puzzle," she began, "but one of the solutions I'm not really sure about. Who is this 'Bin Laden' person?" I had been reading of this 'world's most wanted criminal' in the newspaper, and had chosen to include him as an answer in a puzzle.

The date of my mum's call? September 10, 2001.

But the FBI never called.

Similar stories from the *Guardian*, which has a policy of allowing living people to appear – as opposed to policy at *The Times*, where only The Queen can get a mention – include:

1 My inclusion of a puzzle about UK political also-rans the Monster Raving Loony Party – the day after the puzzle went to press the party's leader, Screaming Lord Sutch, was found dead. He had hanged himself.

2 A reference by Bunthorne to the British painter Patrick Heron, who died on the date of the puzzle's publication.

3 A mention by the setter John Young, aka Shed, of Indian leader Indira Gandhi, the puzzle being published two days after her assassination.

The Times policy being what it is, two or three years back I had just completed the filling of a grid, and was preparing to write the clues. One particular entry had been the US writer and acerbic wit GORE VIDAL. His inclusion had been merited on account of the beautiful structure of the word. GORE VIDAL is: DIVER backwards inside the word GOAL, and seemed perfect for a cryptic clue. But then to my horror I seemed to remember he was still in the land of the living. A quick Google confirmed my fears, and quite intensive surgery on the puzzle ensued in order to remove him.

It is perhaps unkind to feel so disappointed on the discovery of such a luminary's unfortunate state of continuing animation.

MORE POLITICS

During the 2006 Israel-Hezbollah War, the Lebanese city of Tyre was attacked with airstrikes by Israel. Around that time I found myself with the answer 'Spare Tyre' for which to write a clue. Considering that 'Spare Tyre' may also be defined by the flab around one's middle, the clue ended up as:

'Extra weight carried by plea from bombarded Lebanese citizens? (5,4)'.

Some time later, at the Cheltenham Literary Festival, I happened to be in the audience for a talk on the magic of crosswords. A man a few seats in front of me stood up and quoted my clue, asking the panel if political views such as this were acceptable. He considered they weren't. He was an Israeli, and perhaps he was right to be upset but essentially my clue was just a clue, and 'spare tyre' had lent itself to a topical reference. Was it unwise? Possibly. Was it entertaining? Well, many in the audience laughed, but nowadays I am a little more careful. I had evidently offended him, and that had not been my intention.

It seems that one step beyond opinion is the 'definition' of a word. Definitions are loaded. They are set in stone, and supposedly unquestionable. So when crossword setters misjudge them or simply get them wrong, something deep within the human psyche is stirred.

And it is perhaps also the desire to right wrongs, and to appear cleverer than the setter (which more often than not they are) that has many crossword fans penning letters of disgust at our incompetence to periodicals across the globe.

But what is it about politics and crosswords?

Back in Britain, a clue that at the time of writing is awaiting editorial approval:

1 'Some dictatorial bastard from the right (5)'

may well prove to be a little too much, though it was appreciated by the *Guardian* readers on which it was tested.

And do people solve a certain crossword because of its politics? I think traditionally people of particular political persuasions have gravitated towards the aligning periodicals. Crossword editors and setters alike have then aligned their writing with that political stance, or else (in most cases) chosen to avoid politics altogether.

Policy at *The Times* is, probably wisely, to steer clear of controversy. Editors feel their crossword policy should be consistent with their readership. But somehow, more than any other British national newspaper, the *Guardian* has gravitated towards allowing setters more leeway on 'opinion', the newspaper's Arachne recently penning the clue:

2 Throw shoe – bugger the invader of Iraq (6,4)

A SLIGHT PROBLEM

Given the reference to the former British PM mentioned some moments ago, when exactly does a clue become libellous?

Australian night-club owner and property developer Abe Saffron was so upset at a crossword clue in the *Gold Coast Bulletin*'s crossword that he took the newspaper to court for defamation.

The clue, 'Sydney underworld figure, nicknamed Mr Sin (3,7)' according to his lawyer had caused his client to be 'greatly injured in his character, credit and reputation and has been brought into public hatred, ridicule and contempt'.

The newspaper was found guilty on one count of defamation, that of defining him as an 'underworld figure', but not guilty on the second, that of calling him 'Mr Sin'.

SOME PLEASING ANAGRAMS

Aside from 'Presbyterians' becoming BRITNEY SPEARS, there are few stars whose names may be unscrambled from one word. Here are four (answers at the back of the book):

1 Costumier – actor
2 Ablutions – athlete
3 Germany – actress
4 Narcoleptic – musician

A few years ago the BBC radio station 5 live asked listeners to come up with an anagram of a tennis player. The best anagram would win tickets to the Men's Singles Final at Wimbledon.

This author failed miserably. Emptying the Scrabble bag upon my desk, very quickly the former Yugoslav grunter MONICA SELES became 'Camel noises'. However, I submitted only one entry, considering a more impressive effort – there are no E's but 2 V's in the name MARTINA NAVRATILOVA – to be 'Variant rival to a man'. The radio presenters said they considered it to be a little unkind. The winner of the Wimbledon tickets? Another entrant who had independently come up with 'Camel noises'.

Purloined from the online 'Anagram Hall of Fame' page on wordsmith.org, here are a few other anagrams (some of which you may have seen before), which unscramble to form pretty neat, and often relevant, answers.

5 Eleven plus two (three words)
6 They see (two words)
7 Moon starer
8 The classroom
9 Flutter by
10 Near halfwit (three words, hyphenated)
11 I'm a dot in place (two words)
12 Bad credit (two words)

LONG ANAGRAMS

Back in the 1990s, the *Guardian* setter John Henderson, aka Enigmatist, and I had a (fairly) amicable anagram competition between us. It was about who could work the longest anagram into a national newspaper's crossword. I know for a fact that getting mine of 77 letters into one of the *Guardian* grids took around two days. These are the sorts of things we do as setters. For example, it once took me (working off and on) three years to fill a grid with words all of which contained at least one 'Z' – only to find I'd misspelt the Florentine art gallery 'Uffizi' as 'Uffizzi', and my puzle had lost its sizle. It was in the days before crossword software and it took some months to fill it again.

Here was my effort at a long one:

> Here 'n' there in the heavens' watery mire are tiny slits, so the harsh weather is slight, not bulky?

This unravels as a favourite poem from my childhood, entitled *Rain*, by the king of modern British comedy, Spike Milligan. It goes like this:

THERE ARE HOLES IN THE SKY WHERE THE RAIN GETS IN, BUT THEY'RE EVER SO SMALL, THAT'S WHY RAIN IS THIN.

But John was soon to beat me by some way with his, with his 91-letter:

> Seek to protect footloose and fancy-free throne transportation: Roger Miller's to stop loafing one night into drifting

Which works out as the opening lines and title of the 1964 song by Roger Miller:

TRAILER FOR SALE OR RENT,
ROOMS TO LET, FIFTY CENTS,
NO PHONE, NO POOL, NO PETS,
AIN'T GOT NO CIGARETTES
KING OF THE ROAD

And although shorter than ours, I am still in awe at a couple of beauties from Araucaria.

His clue: 'Poetical scene has surprisingly chaste Lord Archer vegetating' yielded, from an anagram of 'chaste Lord Archer vegetating', the solution THE OLD VICARAGE, GRANTCHESTER. The title of a poem by Rupert Brooke, it was also at the time of writing was the home address of the author (Lord) Jeffrey Archer, 'lying' low there after a sex scandal.

Another extraordinary anagram from Araucaria's is 'O, hark the herald angels sing, the boy's descent which lifted up the world'. This unscrambles to WHILE SHEPHERDS WATCH THEIR FLOCKS BY NIGHT ALL SEATED ON THE GROUND. Not only extraordinary for there being the first line of a similar carol in the anagram, but let's consider the second line of the 'While Shepherds' carol:

'The angel of the Lord came down and glory shone around'

– this pretty much described by 'the boy's descent which lifted up the world'.

And here's a classic from American Cory Calhoun, without which a section on long anagrams would be incomplete:

In one of the Bard's best-thought-of tragedies our insistent hero, Hamlet, queries on two fronts about how life turns rotten

This becomes, incredibly:

TO BE OR NOT TO BE: THAT IS THE QUESTION, WHETHER 'TIS NOBLER IN THE MIND TO SUFFER THE SLINGS AND ARROWS OF OUTRAGEOUS FORTUNE ...

OBSCURITIES
'TUTTOQQORTOOQ'

What on earth? Is it:

A An Alaskan petrol-driven raft
B The second language of the Iroquois
C An island of Greenland
D Malagasy for 'Who cares?'

Firstly, I am concerned there are alternative spellings. I have chosen the easier of those. Second, should one be expected to know that this is another name for Deer Island, Greenland? Third, who the heck's heard of Deer Island anyhow? Please forgive me if you have!

So what should one be reasonably be expected to know? I think people feel cheated when the rules of the game are broken. With most puzzles you know what you are getting. The very nature of a closely-interlocking US puzzle is that you will get obscurities. Will Shortz makes clear in his rules for setting a *New York Times* crossword that obscure solutions shouldn't interlock such that you cannot complete the puzzle. In British-style grids it is easier to avoid arcane stuff, so setters should have no excuse.

SCHOOLBOY HUMOUR

For those of you of a delicate disposition, please turn the page now. Or tear this page out, and use it either to light the fire or apply it to your nether regions, whichever you consider more appropriate.

For crosswords, especially the cryptic variety, do lend themselves to the occasional scatological reference, or to moments of juvenility of which I have been probably justly accused.

In fact, my esteemed boss at the *Guardian*, Hugh Stephenson, recently returned one of my puzzles with the exasperated comment "Tthere were two instances of piss and one of shit in this puzzle. I have removed one piss."

The *Daily Mail* once picked up on a puzzle I had sneaked past our battered hero Hugh containing words in which I'd secreted a number of post-watershed words and phrases. This crossword has become known as the 'Scunthorpe Puzzle' (I did warn you), and was inspired by a (possibly apocryphal) story I'd heard about that particular English town in North Lincolnshire whose local council had set up a website in order to attract tourists to the area. The council went live, only to wait, and wait … and wait for someone, just someone to contact them. No one came.

It was only then that it was pointed out that during the setup of the website a filter had been added to remove all vulgarities. Of course, any inquiry containing the key word 'Scunthorpe' was instantly being deleted.

The Scunthorpe puzzle featured the partially unwholesome entries HOT WATER, MISHIT, CHARDONNAY, HORSEMEN and the less subtle WIDOW TWANKEY. The *Daily Mail*, a long term adversary of those tree-huggers at the *Guardian* went characteristically apoplectic at the smut and filth in this '*left-wing*' newspaper, writing a piece explaining 'Cross words…' [titter] '… have been exchanged at the *Guardian*', going on to list a random selection of words from the crossword, some guilty, others innocent, but all SCREAMING IN CAPITALS.

Looking at the piece, for the life of me I cannot see any innuendo in the word ELECTION.

But perhaps the solving public is getting used to a certain barrel-scraping level of conduct on my part.

I recently received a letter from a gentleman who had been solving a clue in the *Guardian* that read:

1 Misshapen genitals, funny things (3,5)

and had confidently entered ODD BALLS.

Here's another: 'Cooler US state, the bottom of America (5)' may give you FAN + NY, but is 'fanny' funny? English and American-English are not always an ocean apart – sometimes it's but an inch.

At the time of writing fast approaching her 100th birthday, *New York Times* puzzle constructor Bernice Gordon recalls how, back in the 1940s, the first editor of the *NYT* 'once changed KREMLIN to GREMLIN, presumably', she says, 'the lesser of two evils; and that another early editor deleted HOSPITAL from a puzzle, as it was 'too gloomy'.

"I do know that we are not allowed to use various parts of the body as such," she adds.

And 'Boob' must be defined as the comic book character McNutt. And a tit is a small bird.'

Indeed it is.

But it is far better to be safe than sorry in the upper chest department, as I was once reminded by a clue from the late great setter Bunthorne:

2 Bird, but not a blue tit (9).

AAARRGGHHH!

Bald crossword solvers in 1940 were surely glad of it, for they had no further hair to tear out.

That year, author and caricaturist Sir Max Beerbohm wrote to *The Times* suggesting that they print a crossword with completely meaningless clues. To "put the solvers in good heart and make them confident of success", Beerbohm included a handful of genuine clues to give solvers the confidence to continue.

Impossible clues included:

'There's a little company in the meadow next month (10)'

and

'A nudist's aunt? (6)'.

Fearful of a backlash, *The Times* published Beerbohm's letter alongside the puzzle.

BLETCHLEY PARK RECRUITMENT

During World War II, brilliant minds were needed to decrypt the ciphers and codes of the Axis powers at the UK's Government Code and Cipher School, based at Bletchley Park, Buckinghamshire.

And what better way to recruit than to select those able to decipher the *Daily Telegraph* crossword in under 12 minutes?

A competition was set up by the newspaper, after which successful entrants were contacted and asked if they would be prepared to undertake a "particular type of work as a contribution to the war effort".

The competition itself was won by F.H.W. Hawes of Dagenham, Essex, who finished in under eight minutes.

And finally, no book covering crossword history can be complete without perhaps the most famous crossword story of them all ...

THE D-DAY LANDINGS CROSSWORDS

June 6, 1944. The Allied forces carry out possibly the most daring operations in military history on the shores of France, following months of planning and a body swerve to convince Hitler that the landings would take place further north up the coast. But ironically, it was one of Britain's most famous meticulously planned deceptions that could have scuppered the whole thing, the deception that is the *Daily Telegraph* crossword.

In the weeks leading up to the operation the word UTAH made an appearance as a solution in the crossword, the codename for the D-Day beach assigned to the 4th Assault Division.

Soon after, OMAHA appeared, codename for another D-Day beach. Coincidences? Maybe.

But then, three more were to follow: OVERLORD (May 27), codename for the whole operation; MULBERRY (May 30), codename for the floating harbours, and on June 1 came NEPTUNE, code for the naval attack phase.

Officials at MI5 were getting jumpy. Not least because they had investigated the appearance of DIEPPE in the puzzle two years earlier, 48 hours before the raid on Dieppe, though their conclusion on that occasion was that this was simply a coincidence.

But that was one word, and this was a whole string of 'coincidences'. Leonard Dawe, setter of all these puzzles was soon to receive a knock on his door from the intelligence services.

It was only in 1984 that a Wolverhampton property manager, Ronald French, came forward and described how as a teenager at Strand School, which had been evacuated to Surrey, he and other pupils had been asked as a mental discipline to fill in blank crossword grids belonging to their headmaster, one Leonard Dawe.

Apparently those particular words had been mentioned by Canadian and American soldiers nearby, and overheard. French, who said he had been hanging around the camp and running errands for the soldiers, claimed that those words were well-known, but that crucially the precise date of the landings remained secret.

Although Dawe was interrogated for some time, MI5 eventually decided that the matter was entirely innocent, and no action was taken against him.

CHAPTER 12
CROSSWORD FANS

JANE BOM-BANE

Jane is arguably the most popular and loved human being in my home city of Brighton and Hove. She is also an acclaimed regular performer at the Edinburgh Festival.

While always busy, she just has to have her daily crossword fix. I'll let her bubbly nature speak for itself:

"Jane Bom-Bane tiddly-ane Fi-Fane, Fi-fane tiddly-ane, that's how you spell Jane."

"I opened the window and in flew Enza!"

When these are the first two things you remember anyone saying to you, you're bound to grow up playing with words.

But you have to be Jane Proper Name till you open your own café, call it Bom-Bane's, then do what you want in it. You can call cocktails Tequila Mockingbird and Tonic Boom, invent words or put Bom- in front of special Bangers and Burgers.

Whenever you like, you can sing palindromic songs you wrote about things going round one way then the other, and put on your RotatoR hat to match.

Or you can invite various artists to adorn all your café doors in black and white to form a crossword trail, then invite customers in to follow it whilst tucking into a snack box of black and white food.'

Jane had asked 20 local artist-customers, from two to 92 years of age, to participate. The results were varied and magnificent.

On each door were three pockets of clues corresponding to three black-and-white themed crosswords (kids', quick and cryptic). After listening to a brief health and safety chat, families of four, single solvers, curious couples and peeping passers-by were let loose in her property to enjoy the doors and the treasure hunt.

When they'd found all 20 clues, they sat in the café with their black and white boxes containing black and white lunch, and set about solving their puzzles in an atmosphere of fun, absorption and determination.

The long-term result is a monthly crossword trail now held at Bom-Bane's.

"I asked my sister Andie if she would write the cryptic one for me," says Jane.

Andie Johnson, who lives in the US, says that, "It was a challenge just to come up with 20 black and white things, let alone clue them cryptically, but I had great fun in the process!"

Andie adds that "the focus, challenge and satisfaction of solving crosswords provide not only absorbing entertainment, but also, during bleaker periods, a reason to keep going."

A couple of examples of Andie's clues:

1 Original piece in concert for northern players (9, 6)
2 What size brassière accommodates this beast? (5)

ROB HUGHES

Stand-up comedian, publisher, 'How To Solve' teacher and general crossword nut, Rob Hughes explains his love for the game:

"I don't know if I'm an obsessive or not, but what might be a closer description would be the Australian term 'tragic', an affectionate word for someone who knows more about something than general social skills should allow for – for example, 'the foreign secretary and noted cricket tragic'."

Rob explains his love for the cryptic crossword:

"The joys of those puzzles are myriad.

"They have a unique solution that you reach using a combination of a given set of rules and your own creativity. They appeal to my love of language, they test my creativity, vocabulary, lateral thinking and empathy all at the same time, whilst being uniquely comforting.

"I also like the esoteric nature of them, different rules for different papers and I think if I laugh out loud once a week from a clue the setters are doing well. It can be the elegance of the clue, a particularly fiendish bit of misdirection, a beautiful incongruity between the surface reading and the answer, anything really.

"Feather-spitting wise I'm actually fairly tolerant, but I do get grumpy with clues that are barely cryptic at all (for example anagrams where you just have to move one letter) and some of the more tortured, Spoonerisms.

"But *Listener* crosswords might as well be written in Linear B for all the sense I can make of them."

Rob adds some thoughts on what he would consider cheating:

"To my mind, buying a "how to solve cryptic crosswords" book or a Crossword solver's dictionary or book of Crossword lists would be cheating, but then I am both completely self-taught and ridiculously hard on myself. I don't really understand the 'check' and 'cheat' buttons on the online versions. How desperate can anyone be to know? The answers are only a day away, for God's sake. I always do them in pen – not pencil (have the courage of your convictions!) Actually I use pens for solving and pencils for the puzzles I am learning to set. I do recourse to reference books and of course the Internet, but only to verify answers I've already worked out (or think I have). I would not, however, think anyone else was cheating if they did any of the above. They are only crossword puzzles, after all!"

CHAPTER 13
CELEBRITY SOLVERS

BRIAN WILSON

San Francisco Giants closing baseball pitcher Brian Wilson is noted for his flamboyant personality.

He has been fined for his attire of bright orange cleats. Wilson has sported a Mohawk and has tanned his extended facial hair, eliciting chants from Giants fans of 'Fear the beard'. Furthermore, in an interview with US sports talk show host Jim Rome in 2012, Brian claimed to be a Certified Ninja after taking 12 minutes to pass all the necessary courses in a dream.

But when it comes to taking his rock star personality up just one more notch, Brian Wilson is a devoted crossword nut, having been tackling the *New York Times* crossword from the age of 12.

And just days before striking out Texas slugger Nelson Cruz for the World Series win, he declared publicly that he would like to be in a crossword clue one day, preferably in a clue that was "down, not across, as the down ones are usually harder."

Wilson's dream of finally appearing in black and white came true in 2011, appearing at 30 Down as 'Giants hurler (2010 champs)/Beach Boys vocalist on "Help Me Rhonda" (#1 in 1965)' in a puzzle written by constructors Tyler Hinman and Jeremy Horwiz. The crossword was based on baseball pitchers who had won World Series, and who shared names with musicians with #1 billboard hits. You wouldn't think there were any beyond Wilson. But DAVE STEWART, EDDIE FISHER and KENNY ROGERS also fitted the bill.

SOPHIE WINKLEMAN

Acclaimed stage and TV comedy actress, and Big Suze in the UK cult hit *Peep Show*, Sophie Winkleman talks of her love for her puzzle of choice.

"A great cryptic crossword is a great friend. You can while away the hours with this friend; in turn captivated, amused, seduced, challenged, delighted, maddened and educated by the hypnotic square in front of you.

"Have a fan explain the basic rules ('new' often denotes an anagram, the solution nearly always means the first or last bit of the clue not the middle, 'queen' is usually 'er', etc), start practising (finding out the solutions if you're stuck and working out why they're correct) and voila! You will not be bored, restless or lonely ever again.

"A great crossword is also a great escape in that you simply cannot think about anything else when trying to solve. What better therapy could there be?

"The cryptic crossword is like a tantric boudoir for the brain – it teases, tickles, tantalizes, pummels, stretches, broadens, and opens your mind like nothing else.

"You enter the lair of the setter, an instant tourist, picking up his language, his laws, his codes, his humour, his mores. It is a deeply intimate experience.

"You start knowing the setters' individual countries – so when it's a Paul you know you're off to a madly funny, ingenious wonderland where bra straps are twanged and elves roll spliffs in the woods. Araucaria takes you to *A Midsummer Night's Dream* of enchantment, Tramp to a thumping house party, Rufus to a hammock beneath an apple tree. The setters become familiar and well-loved friends – maddening you and thrilling you in equal measure.

"A crossword is the best companion for any stretch of time – a dinner, a flight, a train journey, or to be addressed at intervals throughout the day. I cannot imagine life without the cryptic crossword, the most enriching thread of my life's fabric, and the best gift my parents could have given me."

RICK EDWARDS

Thirty-something Channel 4 and E4 presenter, Cambridge graduate and ex-model, Rick Edwards is as cool as they come. Which is why he loves crosswords.

"My love of crosswords stems, I guess, from my parents.

"My mum in particular has a seemingly endless supply of crossword puzzle books that she sits with in the lounge, quietly completing, pretty much every night. Only pausing occasionally to shout a clue at my father, who always seems to know the answer without looking up from his paper. Infuriating.

"My appetite for crosswords is similarly ravenous. I will do any and every crossword that I come across(word). Quick, cryptic, it doesn't matter. I scoop up discarded papers on public transport, pen-twitching. There are few feelings more satisfying than a completed grid. I always finish with a flourish – a massive tick across the whole thing. Done. I had a brief flirtation with Sudoku puzzles, but it never came to anything. My heart remains with the crossword.

"I'm not sure that I could successfully list all of the various clue-types,' Rick continues, 'but fundamentally I enjoy clues that have baffled me for ages, before suddenly becoming clear. I always enjoy an anagram – and fancy myself to be pretty good at them – and also the ones where the solution is made up of words within words, if that makes sense.

"My favourite clue is the old …

1 HIJKLMNO (5)?

"…which I know infuriates purists but appeals to me. It is a classic riddle."

For those of you who haven't seen this before, it's a 'say what you see' sort of clue.

JO BRAND

Jo Brand is one of Britain's best-known alternative comedy stand-ups.

Much like many comics whose tool of the trade is the play-on-words, Jo loves her crosswords.

While letting me know she is 'on my case' in the *Guardian*, Jo offered these thoughts on her favourite, and most distracting, hobby:

"Who are these cruciverbalists with their grids of torment who unsettle my composure – who invade the grey substance of my brain and squeeze out, drop by drop, the last vestiges of my word retrieval skills to solve their capricious clues?

"I only sat down for five minutes – an hour later, coffee cold, work plans shot.

"Crosswords are a source of satisfaction and wonder, and a little thief of precious time."

WILL SHORTZ

Since he has also appeared as a character on *The Simpsons*, and in the film *Wordplay*, it is surely *New York Times* Crossword Editor Will Shortz who has had the most brushes with crossword celebrities, interviewing US entertainment business magnate Merv Griffin, multi-award-winning composer and lyricist Stephen Sondheim, and the then presidential candidate Bill Clinton. During their encounter Clinton timed himself on a puzzle of medium difficulty, and in under seven minutes it was complete.

CHAPTER 14
MY HERO – ARAUCARIA

Raised in Oxford, his father Eric being Dean of Oriel College, the young John Graham headed to Cambridge to study classics at King's College.

Studies were interrupted by the onset of war in Europe and, joining the RAF, he was to bail out over Italy, being rescued by the Americans and gaining a mention in despatches.

Returning to King's to study theology, and soon to become a vicar, he later took up puzzling, writing his first for the *Guardian* in 1958. In 1970, when the newspaper asked its setters to take pseudonyms, John opted for the Latin for the monkey-puzzle tree, 'Araucaria', under which name he has been delighting solvers ever since.

On January 11, 2013 he announced to the world via a preamble accompanying *Guardian* Cryptic Crossword No. 25842 that: "Araucaria has 18 down of the 19, which is being treated with 13 15". Upon unravelling the puzzle, it would become clear that Araucaria was being treated with palliative care for oesophagal cancer.

Many who solved the puzzle said they cried while doing so, for although they perhaps hadn't had the opportunity to meet him in person, they had certainly grown to regard him as a great friend. As had I.

Summer 1994: on receiving my first attempt at a puzzle, Araucaria had invited me to meet him for lunch. I had not yet even been published, and here was generosity from my hero beyond my wildest dreams.

The Rev. John Graham has been described as the living Shakespeare. I was painfully anxious and sick with nerves. Furthermore, through characteristic foolishness I had over-celebrated after acquiring a Teaching English as a Foreign Language (TEFL) certificate the previous night. My head was pounding, and nausea had set in. On top of this, and to my horror having promised to buy him lunch, holes-in-the-wall around London were not supplying any money. I had just enough to take the train from King's Cross north to Huntingdon, where the great man would be awaiting me on the platform. Araucaria would end up having to pay for my lunch – the shame of it – but I did reimburse him later.

At 26 years old, and an immature 26, I was short on self-confidence, but in my heart I knew I deserved this chance. I'd worked extraordinarily hard to get this far, seven days a week, from the moment of waking, way beyond the burning of the midnight oil. One honed puzzle had been written. Just to meet him.

I boarded the train at King's Cross, settled myself, and the train pulled away. It had left two minutes early.

I glanced at my watch. Trains were not meant to depart early, especially in Britain. Trains were supposed to be at least ten minutes late.

49. Araucaria
The Guardian, April 2013

ACROSS

1 27 of 6s? (7)

5 Oath to the French king, one interrupting speech (7)

9 Free love – have no success without it (5)

10 You snivel unpleasantly, wishing you were me? (9)

11 Put in letters for ice-breaker keeping weapon (9)

12 Do this to cite this for 11 (5)

13 Make music, including Western music (5)

15 Coster from Furness (6,3)

18 Ship's first come into old one's bell and pursued it with vigour (9)

19 Get rid of land on sea (5)

21 See 20 Down

23 Supply lamps the ginnel needed ... (9)

25 ... and heater fit needed in Soviet city (9)

26 See 27

27/26 Caesar's bulls forged? So what? (3,4,2,3)

28 Did the 6 – or was unable to? (7)

DOWN

1 You translated poetry on the Sun (7)

2 Fwightful cwimes without a subject of novel tale (3,6)

3 What happened to regular model? (5)

4 Pole, expert with ball, keeping it up, having an easy name? (9)

5 Hard part of wader's cry to 9 '27 26' (5)

6 This could bar you from the Dunmow flitch (9)

7 Girl to love catcher? (5)

8 Tory shambles containing rising of the people – top people (7)

14 Dormouse gets sulphur and oxygen on a sliding scale, perhaps (9)

16 Quickly collected red coat and organized duel quietly (7,2)

17 From abbey to cathedral (almost) in Somerset – it's much drier (4,5)

18 Was stretched out on the ground fatally wounded (3,4)

20/21 German one of 27 brings up, without colouring, time 26 between 1s (7,5)

22 Musical gunner in a pub raised a point (5)

23 Wind once blowing from Europe to America? (5)

24 German/American artist given a little Polish money (5)

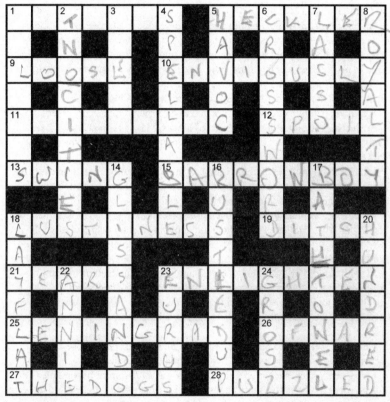

First published in the *Guardian* newspaper.

The horror – I was on the wrong train.

Head in hands and close to tears at my own incompetence, I knew not whether I was bound for Liverpool or Glasgow – and had I missed my chance to meet him, and my only chance for a career I would enjoy?

A handful of desperate minutes passed, before which the train pulled in at the first stop, Finchley Road, at which I quickly jumped from the train. To my relief, the correct train pulled in a couple of minutes later on the adjacent platform, and suddenly I was on course again.

An hour later, arriving at Huntingdon, I crossed the footbridge and, wobble-kneed, descended the steps towards him. This was not how it was meant to be. The approach should not have been from on high, but from below, genuflecting to drop at his feet and worship him. How dare I swoop down on him like a vulture?

Stepping from the stairs, paces away, I was relieved to see that he was taller than me. I also remember his elegance, and his startling blue eyes.

We shook hands, exchanged smiles and I was ushered to his car, a Fiat Uno.

Reality had just hit. A Fiat Uno? Here He was, Master of the Cruciverbal Universe – driving a Fiat Uno. It was at that moment I came to terms with the fact that I would always be poor.

John Graham proved a delight. I remember little of our conversation over lunch in a local pub, my head being in a bubble, but remain in awe of him to this day, despite the great man's utter humility and friendliness.

Araucaria was more than an avuncular figure. At the age of eighteen I had lost my father. My grandfather and, shockingly, my brother too were to fall in the next handful of years. In my head I adopted him as the male head of the family, for I needed him.

And I treasured his effortlessly crafted and good-natured letters over the following years in which he attempted to steer me towards good cluing techniques, and away from shocking girlfriend choices. In correspondence, he would be addressed as J/A, as I was unsure whether 'John' or 'Araucaria' worked as alternatives.

Here was someone to take care of me, to guide me through those difficult years of loss and often isolation. I cannot thank him enough.

Many years later, we are on hugging terms, and I love him beyond measure.

And recently I was fortunate enough to be able to email Araucaria to tell him that the puzzle on the previous page, published in April 2013, reminded me why I first fell in love with crosswords.

I do hope you enjoy it.

SECTION 5
ONLINE SOLVING COMMUNITIES
AND TECHNOLOGY

POWER SHIFT

Top US constructor and solver Tyler Hinman says the balance of power is shifting away from the newspapers and towards the creators of the puzzles.

"More and more puzzle projects are cropping up on Kickstarter – a website on which creative people set a funding goal and deadline for their project, and if people like that project they can pledge money to make it happen. More puzzle projects are also appearing through individual constructors' websites.

"It's really given many puzzle-makers an escape from submitting to newspapers and magazines, which frequently buy all rights to a puzzle for a mediocre amount of money, meaning it can be perpetually reprinted without its author seeing another dime."

PUZZLE ACCESSIBILITY

A Royal National Institute of Blind People member and volunteer, and 3-D crossword designer who is registered blind, Eric Westbrook is most definitely a visionary. Here he explains what the future holds, crossword-wise, for the visually impaired:

"The Smartphone is rapidly becoming the centre of communications and entertainment for people with visual impairment.

"The next two years will 'see', or rather hear, accessible crosswords using manual entries on touch screen keyboards on phones. Voice activated applications will follow and sighted solvers will join in.

"We are looking into various uses of electronic grids, and surely we are not far down the road from the utilization of sensory extensions and bionics."

And early this year Sam Twidale, an undergraduate student at the University of York, developed a program allowing the blind to solve Eric's 3-D crosswords, puzzles which are built a little like blocks of flats, where clues are solved in 'Across', 'Away' and 'Down' directions.

The program allows users to select crossword clues, which the Speech Application Programming Interface (SAPI) on their computer then reads out.

Any words that are not clear, are ambiguous or are homophones, will be audibly read out. The solver types their answers using the keyboard and these are recorded visually in the grid and the table of clues.

Solvers can move to clues affected by solutions to hear any letters that already appear in the grid. In this way, the program gives the blind solver the same information that the sighted puzzler could gain from looking at the crossword grid.

CROSSWORDS ALL OVER THE WORLD

David Astle, arguably the biggest name in Australasian puzzledom, says:

"Websites, Twitter, blogs and chat rooms have given real momentum to crossword culture in Australia. The far-flung corners of the island can now unite to celebrate and/or nitpick a single puzzle. While chances to publish are slim compared to the UK and US, the solving scene is booming thanks to social media.

"Add to this the spread of crossword-solving courses at tertiary colleges, the access to quality puzzles offshore, plus the increasing growth of the Australian Crossword Club, and you sense the devotion across the nation."

And this is happening all over the world. Community is forming: wherever you are on the planet, if you have the crossword bug, you now have access to a community. While you can choose to solve alone or with a friend, there is now a huge, and growing, global bond between those with a love of the cruciverbal art.

COMMUNITY AND FRIENDSHIP

Fan turned crossword creator Neil Walker, aka Tramp in the *Guardian,* looks at how the Worldwide Web has brought setters and solvers closer together.

"In many respects, the future of crosswords has never looked rosier. Advances in technology and, in particular, the Internet have enabled solvers and setters to correspond with each other to form one big, generally happy crossword family.

"Back in the '90s, when I started solving puzzles, I was absolutely fascinated by these magical setters whose pseudonyms appeared in the *Guardian*. I had no idea what the setting process involved and was fascinated how anyone could manage to fill a grid with *real* words, let alone incorporating several thematically linked words into the same grid, or anagrams could be found that seemed too good to be true.

"I would wonder what these setters looked like, what they wore, whether they had jobs, whether they had secret handshakes or exposed their nipples in public. I longed to correspond with these people. I remember reading an article explaining that Bunthone used to be a TV presenter, that Enigmatist was a psychology lecturer, Araucaria a churchman and that Shed was Audreus's son. I couldn't get enough of this hot gossip; for me, this information was like Posh and Becks's bedroom to an *OK!* reader.

"When Paul asked for donations for his charity trip to Peru under one Saturday puzzle, I used the charity address and sent a note hoping that it would get passed to him: years later, having met him, he told me that he found my note under a pile of books. It's hard to imagine those days now, and I'm only talking about the 1990s.

"Nowadays, through the excellent sites like the *Guardian* comments site, fifteensquared.net, Derek Harrison's Crossword Site, Times for the Times, Big Dave's Crossword Blog, Alan Connor's weekly blog on the *Guardian* website, to name just a few, crosswords are analysed (sometimes over-analysed) and dissected and the barrier between setter and solver has disappeared.

"Many setters have their own websites (Anax, Brummie, Paul, to name but a few) and social gatherings are organized where setters and solvers can get together and enjoy a drink or two. In some ways, losing the mysticism is a shame but having the friends that I have made through crosswords is amazing.

"I would say that there are more top-notch setters now than at any time in the past, many of them (Donk, Picaroon, Qaos and Rorschach, for example) are barely out of nappies – some of them might not even be out of nappies – but with these setters' brilliant work coupled with the accessibility to puzzles improving all the time and with the community getting ever stronger, I think the future of the crossword is in good hands.

"I have two daughters (aged five and three). They see me try to solve crosswords, and they watch as I sit at the computer for hours trying to write them; and they ask questions such as 'when are you going to feed us?' for example, but all jesting aside I'm hoping they pick up the crossword bug by osmosis.

"I would encourage any reader with younger members of the family to try their hardest to get them to see the joy of crosswords – after all, if you were born on a desert island with nobody to show you how to read, look at the joy you would miss out on. So with that in mind, let's all make it a goal to mentor a solver and introduce them to the Joy of X(words): the best fun you can have with your pants on (although you're free to take them off if it helps – I know I sometimes do)."

DIGITAL VS NEWSPRINT – WHICH DO YOU PREFER?

For me, nothing will ever beat having the good old-fashioned newspaper on a café table, solving with a black biro. Even a printout doesn't quite do it – and you can't scribble notes on an iPhone app.

The newspapers won't admit it, but I believe that our love of solving the crossword on a folded newspaper is what is keeping the papers alive around the world.

And long may it continue.

THE FUTURE – THE VISION

We often consider the crossword a humble puzzle – humble it is not.

Our beloved puzzle has survived a century with two world wars, and is known by the vast majority of people on the planet. It is vibrant, and it is thriving.

The crossword has the power to unite people through words – just look at the communities that are growing online all over the world. It has the power to educate, not because we *have* to learn, but because we *choose* to learn.

The crossword is a powerful tool indeed. But this power has not been fully harnessed.

Yet.

As a child, I grew up being frightened of appearing stupid. If I got things wrong, there'd often be unpleasant consequences. I'd be shouted at or called names.

Even today I am sometimes frightened to pick up a book for fear that if I don't understand the plot or a particular phrase, this will be confirmation of my stupidity. Indeed, perhaps you've had a similar experience yourself?

But this doesn't need to happen – to anyone.

What would it be like if we all were free to make mistakes when learning – with a freedom to get it wrong the first, second, third and fourth times, with no loss of power, and no loss of confidence?

In the same way that a child likes to explore something new, how would it be if every child couldn't wait to open a new book, to read and to learn. With a desire to succeed and a sense of adventure, but no fear of failure.

I believe this is possible.

The power to create this comes through the mightiest weapon we hold – our own language.

Words express our love, our fear. They are our access to friendships and relationships. Wars begin at the word of a military commander; and they end at the signing of a peace declaration.

If a child puts his hand up in class to give the teacher the answer, only to be told the answer is wrong, that child may hear sniggers around the classroom.

On hearing them, the child decides it's safer not to try again for fear of looking stupid, and keeps their arm firmly down, perhaps forever.

And fearful children become fearful adults; afraid to communicate, afraid to contribute – and alone. Let's end that fear.

Let's play a game. Let's make educational puzzles and games that become part of everyday life for children – and create them in such a way that getting the wrong answer is just part of the journey, and not the end.

And let it be fun – let's leave the child always acknowledged, and present to their intelligence and capability.

My vision is that:

By December 2018, word games and puzzle solving will form part of school curricula across the world.

Children will be playing with words in a way that leaves them empowered. They will be solving at their own pace – every clue solved being acknowledged.

We'll be talking to leaders in education and government in order to make this happen. I believe it can happen. And I believe it will.

Children will be having fun with words in the school playground, perhaps even writing clues for each other to solve – and puzzles too! It'll be standard practice to be searching for magic within words, start jumbling letters, finding hidden words within words, hidden meanings, delight in discovering that the word BRAVEST is formed from the underwear items 'bra' and 'vest'.

Young people will grow up understanding that they are good with words; that they can express themselves clearly and freely – that words are fun.

And if children see words as fun, they might well be thinking about careers and opportunities that otherwise they may not have considered. Perhaps they might want to become a writer, a journalist – or a teacher.

But dreams remain just dreams – unless we take action.

If, like me, you believe that having fun with words is the access to communication, and to freedom from fear, join me and find out more at:

www.puzzlecommunities.com

50. Prize Puzzle

Solve the puzzle on this page for a chance to win one of five bespoke puzzles by some of the world's greatest puzzle setters/constructors, with clues exclusively written about you and about all your favourite things! See puzzlecommunities.com for details.

Thank you for reading this book. Remember: next time you solve a crossword, feel proud. You are part of something special. You are a member of a friendly and delightful world community that really makes a difference.

You are a crossword solver.

ACROSS

1 One of these (9)
6 Informal or vulgar language (5)
9 Sandy __, *Pretty Girl in Crimson Rose (8)* author (7)
10 One with much experience? (7)
11 Frivolity and fun (6)
12 I'm off! (6-2)
13 Chessman – bird – cheat (4)
14 Most important (9)
18 Language for all? (9)
19 India's continent (4)
23 Faith or confidence (8)
25 You! – lovers (anag) (6)
27 Observer (7)
28 Flowering plant – oil able (anag) (7)
29 Boob (5)
30 Editor's change (9)

DOWN

1 Shoe-mender – pie – drink – dessert (7)
2 Unconscious (9)
3 Will __, *NYT* puzzle giant (6)
4 Giant of folklore (4)
5 Underarm spray or roll-on (9)
6 Lateral way in or way out? (4,4)
7 David __ Australian puzzler supremo (5)
8 Bernice __, veteran *NYT* constructor (6)
15 Monkey-puzzle tree – the *Guardian*'s most-loved setter (9)
16 Tennessee capital (9)
17 Figure of speech (8)
20 Side by side (7)
21 Richard __, *Times* 1 across editor (6)
22 Outlaw (6)
24 Not now! (5)
26 Hint such as this? (4)

SOLUTIONS
ANSWERS TO CLUES:

David Astle's clues:
1 SUGAR-COAT 2 EB WHITE 3 MESSAGE IN A BOTTLE 4 STAGE DOOR 5 GENITALIA
6 NO ANIMAL WAS HURT DURING THE MAKING OF THIS CROSSWORD

Brian Greer's clues:
1 LATIN 2 ARITHMETIC

John Young's clues:
1 POLL TAX 2 AMPUTEE

John Henderson's clues:
1 OFTENTIMES 2 VINDALOO 3 EGO 4 FAST-BREEDER 5 BOTTLE PARTY 6 INEFFABLE
7 BRAINWASH 8 HIDDEN AGENDA 9 MUSH

Rich Norris' team's clues:
1 OIL CARTELS 2 I BEFORE E 3 SNORED 4 URSA 5 ALI BABA 6 ST PETER 7 BEAD CURTAIN
8 BLAB 9 CLIMB 10 ASS 11 BRONCO 12 DENTED 13 KODAK 14 COLANDER 15 ELOPE

Crossword Stories: More Politics:
1 BLAIR 2 GEORGE BUSH

Some Pleasing Anagrams:
1 TOM CRUISE 2 USAIN BOLT 3 MEG RYAN 4 ERIC CLAPTON 5 TWELVE PLUS ONE
6 THE EYES 7 ASTRONOMER 8 SCHOOLMASTER 9 BUTTERFLY 10 FATHER-IN-LAW
11 DECIMAL POINT 12 DEBIT CARD

Schoolboy humour:
1 TAG LINES 2 REDBREAST

Crossword Fans: Andie Johnson:
1 NEWCASTLE UNITED 2 ZEBRA

Rick Edwards:
1 WATER (H to O)

ANSWERS TO CROSSWORDS

Solution No 1.

Solution No 2.

Solution No 3.

Solution No 4.

Solution No 5.

Solution No 6.

Solution No 7.

Solution No 8.

Solution No 9.

Solution No 10.

Solution No 11.

Solution No 12.

Solution No 13.

Solution No 14.

Solution No 15.

Solution No 16.

Solution No 17.

Solution No 18.

Solution No 19.

Solution No 20.

Solution No 21.

Solution No 22.

Solution No 23.

Solution No 24.

Solution No 25.

Solution No 26.

Solution No 27.

Solution No 28.

Solution No 29.

Solution No 30.

Solution No 31.

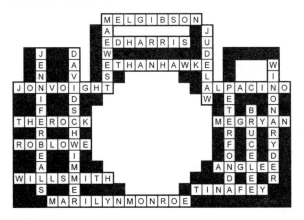

Solution No 32.

Solution No 33.

Solution No 34.

Solution No 35.

Solution No 36.

```
  A P P R E H E N S I O N
P   A   U   U   I   B   O
L U R E D   M A N S I O N
A   V   E   B   E   Z   E
I D E A   E L E P H A N T
N   N   L   E   I       H
S Q U E A L   A N N E X E
A       C   B   S   Y   W
I M M O R T A L   Y E T I
L   A   O   L   S   S   S
I N C I S E D   P R O N E
N   H   S   E   I   R   R
G L O B E T R O T T E R
```

Solution No 37. Cryptic

```
H A S H T A G   M O N G R E L
U   T   A   E   I   U   E   E
M O R T I C E A N D T E N O N
D   A   W   Z   K   T   O   S
R E P L A C E   C R Y O V A C
U   P   N   R   O       A   A
M E E K E R   H A M S I T U P
    D   S   V   T   N   O
B U F F E T E D   B O V R I L
A   O       N   H   W   S   P
C A R Y A R D   I N F I D E L
K   C   T   E   A   L   R   A
R E A L E S T A T E A G E N T
U   S   A   T   U   K   A   E
B O H E M I A   S T E A M E R
```

Solution No 37. Straight

```
S W E E P E R   F R A N T I C
A   A   O   O   R   L   A   A
T H R O W S T H E B O O K A T
S   T   E   U   U   O   E   E
U S H E R I N   D E F I N E R
M   S   G   D   I       O   E
A S H O R E   B A G P I P E R
    A   I   S   N   L   R
A N T I D O T E   J U N I O R
S   T       O   F   R   S   E
P R E V I E W   L E A D O F F
I   R   M   A   U   L   N   U
R A I N B O W L O R I K E E T
I   N   U   A   R   S   R   E
N U G G E T Y   O S M O S I S
```

Solution No 38.

```
B R I T O N   M A N I F O L D
  I   W   A   U   O   R   I
A N T O N Y M S   T R A U M A
  G   T   S   I   A   N   B
      I N A C C U R A C I E S
  T   M   Y   T   I       R
V I L E   O V E R W I N D
  M   R   S   O   S   E   E
R E A S S I G N   L I S T
  S   T   E   K   L   S
N E W B R U N S W I C K
  R   A   A   E   T   N   D
A V O C E T   A S S O O N A S
  E   K   E   R   C   W   I
P R E S I D E S   H A N D L E
```

Solution No 39.

```
D O G ■ W A G O N ■ T R A S H
A A A ■ E R O D E ■ H E L L O
W H E N I M S I X T Y F O U R
G U L A G ■ S E T H ■ ■ O N S
■ ■ S H Y ■ ■ ■ O R A N G E
E I G H T O F C L U B S ■ ■
A D O ■ S W O R E ■ I K N O W
R E A D ■ L O O T S ■ S O B E
P A L E O ■ T A U P E ■ M O E
■ S W E E T S I X T E E N ■
T A P I N S ■ ■ T M I ■
O N O ■ P A T H ■ A D D E R
O N E H U N D R E D Y E A R S
T I M E S ■ J U L I O ■ M I V
H E S H E ■ S E D E R ■ P C P
```

Explanation from Matt Gaffney: the four numbers in theme entries had to be quartered (i.e. multiplied by .25); then you needed to take the first quarter of the resulting clue numbers to spell out a trivia question:

17-a [It mentions the Isle of Wight (first, quarter; then first quarter)] = WHEN I'M SIXTY-FOUR (16)

28-a [Part of the Dead Man's Hand (first, quarter; then first quarter)] = EIGHT OF CLUBS (2)

50-a [NCAA Men's Division I Championship teams who've won their first two games, collectively (first, quarter; then first quarter)] = SWEET SIXTEEN (4)

66-a [Duration of solitude, in a literary title (first, quarter; then first quarter)] = ONE HUNDRED YEARS (25)

Now let's look at those clue numbers in parentheses above, and take the first quarter of them — if they're four words long we'll take the first word, if they're eight words long we'll take the first two words, etc.

16-a ["**What** is it, caller?"]

2-d [**State quarter** with this island's outline? It's Hawaii]

4-d [**Features a** gym is very likely to have]

25-a [**Piece of fruit** that also just happens to be a common color]

What state quarter features a piece of fruit? Why it's **GEORGIA**, the fourth state (appropriately for a puzzle about quarters).

Solution No 40.

Solution No 41.

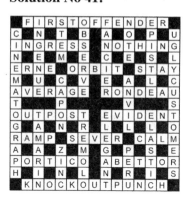

Solution No 42.

Solution No 43.

Solution No 44.

The convention's theme was that the puzzles were lipogrammatic, lacking any Es. This crossword had no Es in the preamble or clues, and all answers were entered with Es removed.

Solution No 45.

Solution No 46.

Solution No 47.

Solution No 48.

Solution No 49.

ACKNOWLEDGEMENTS

Anon (**Onan**) – for the bits on cricket

David Astle (**Slated diva**) – for flying the flag

Sandy Balfour (**Nobly as fraud**) – for being South African, but for supporting the England cricket team

Ken Beveridge (**Keen bed giver**) – for kind hosting

Jane Bom-Bane (**Mean job, babe**) – for the hugs!

Alex Buck (**Luxe back**) – for friendship, and for trusting me

Jo Brand (**Darn job**) – for loving crosswords

Richard Browne (**Wordier branch**) – for exceptional editorship

Shaun Clohessy (**Unholy as chess**) – for love, art and friendship

Vincent Clohessy (**Novelty chicness**) – for outstanding friendship beyond measure

Michael Curl (**Crucial helm**) – for consistent quality and humour

Rick Edwards (**Dick rewards**) – for being far, far too smart

Francesca Elston (**Cleanness factor**) – for great checking, and for biscuits

Anne Erdmann (**Mannered nan**) – for the love of crosswords

Dan Feyer (**Deny fear**) – for genius under pressure

Richard Fletcher (**Fetch rarer child**) – for first-rate and comprehensive research

Matt Gaffney (**Fatten my fag**) – for creating the future

Jenny Glanville (**Jangle evil Lynn**) – for freedom from anxiety

Mark Goodliffe (**Of a milked frog**) – for having a brain the size of a planet

Bernice Gordon (**Cornered bingo**) – for your decades of fun

John Graham (**Mahjong rah**) – for my wonderful life

Brian Greer (**Rarer being**) – for exceptional puzzles

John Grimshaw (**Mahjong whirs**) – for unrelenting quality

Jonathan Hall (**Than all Jonah**) – for exceptional talent and generosity

Roland Hall (**Ran holdall**) – for dedication and for the opportunity

ACKNOWLEDGEMENTS

Anthony Halpern (**Nylon parent – hah**) for loving me

Aram Halpern (**Her nap alarm**) – for my joy

Belle Halpern (**Ban leper hell**) – for the crossword spark

Louise Halpern (**European hills**) – for being a brilliant sister

Margaret Halpern (**Alter her pangram**) – for strength and love, for making me and for growing me up

Paul Halpern (**Allah pre-nup**) – for being my inspiration, always

Alison Hayes (**So any Sheila**) – for sisterly love, and for being a great hostess

Sarah Hayes (**Arsey ha-has**) – for women, and for humour

Ani Haytayan (**A Thai, nay nay**) – for stunning cooking, and for raising a wonderful family

Jirair Haytayan (**Hairy Tirana jay**) – for kindness and smiles

John Henderson (**Her hen's donjon**) – for great puzzles, and for more friendship than I have returned

Tyler Hinman (**I learnt hymn**) – for being at the top of your games

Rob Hughes (**Bores Hugh**) – for being a good bloke

Mike Hutchinson (**Hunk notices him**) – for the pirates

Colin Inman (**Minion clan**) – for your support, and for your supporting Brighton

Jean Johnson (**One's non-Hajj**) – for checking and chuckles

Ashley Knowles (**Yes, he's know-all**) – for supporting the crossword-setting community

Don Manley (**And lemony**) – for your commitment to the cause

Dean Mayer (**Neared May**) – for the riffs

Dave Moore (**Evade room**) – for the love of football and crosswords

Stanley Newman (**Lament any news**) – for bringing power to the people

Rich Norris (**Cirri shorn**) – for your generosity and talent

Kim Osmond (**Sodom mink**) – for wonderful event hosting, and for shouting at cyclists

Kaz Pasiecznik (**Sink pizza cake**) – for bringing cryptic crosswords to the world

Lisa Perry (**Parley, sir**) – for fun and ideas

Roger Phillips (**Shop girl peril**) – for the challenge

Virginia Preston (**Groins in private**) – for great checking, and for cakes

Merl Reagle (**Glam leerer**) – for being pun-tastic

Kay Reynolds (**Nakedly rosy**) – for the love, friendship and support

Helen Roden (**Lend her one**) – for brilliant ideas

Richard Rogan (**Arch or daring**) – for setting the bar high

Will Shortz (**Trolls whiz**) – for brilliance

Roger Squires (**Require gross**) – for humility, talent and kindness

Hugh Stephenson (**Phones, then hugs**) – for your patience

David Stickley (**Valid city desk**) – for a career of making people happy

Nigel Stonier (**Lingerie snot**) – for thinking big, and making it happen

Sue Taylor (**Arsey lout**) – for being a fabulous hostess

Liza Tong (**A long zit**) – for support, drive and delicious food

Shuchismita Upadhyay (**Pity my sad Chihauhuas**) – for brilliant research, and commitment to the cause

Barry Winkleman (**A brawny Kremlin**) – for friendship, incredible support, and for the ability to speak whole sentences backwards

Sophie Winkleman (**Pinkish eel woman**) – for always making my day, and for exuding love and generosity

Arthur Wynne (**Ray threw nun**) – for the crossword

John Young (**Non-joy hug**) – for the generosity of a long lunch break

and

Taline Halpern (**Hi, eternal plan**) – for love, forever

"The nice thing about doing a crossword puzzle is, you know there is a solution."

Stephen Sondheim

There's story connected with how far
it's developed? (3, 9, 2, 3, 9)